BFI Modern Classics

Rob White
Series Editor

Advancing into its second century, the cinema is now a mature art form with an established list of classics. But contemporary cinema is so subject to every shift in fashion regarding aesthetics, morals and ideas that judgments on the true worth of recent films are liable to be risky and controversial; yet they are essential if we want to know where the cinema is going and what it can achieve.

As part of the British Film Institute's commitment to the promotion and evaluation of contemporary cinema, and in conjunction with the influential BFI Film Classics series, BFI Modern Classics is a series of books devoted to individual films of recent years. Distinguished film critics, scholars and novelists explore the production and reception of their chosen films in the context of an argument about the film's importance. Insightful, considered, often impassioned, these elegant, beautifully-illustrated books will set the agenda for debates about what matters in modern cinema.

Once Upon a Time in America

Adrian Martin

Publishing

First published in 1998 by the
British Film Institute
21 Stephen Street, London W1P 2LN

The British Film Institute is the UK national agency with responsibility for encouraging the arts of film and television and conserving them in the national interest.

Series design by Andrew Barron &
Collis Clements Associates

Typeset in Italian Garamond
by D R Bungay Associates, Burghfield, Berks

Picture editing by Millie Simpson

Designed by Tom Cabot

Printed in Great Britain by
Norwich Colour Print, Drayton, Norfolk.

British Library Cataloguing-in-Publication Data
A catalogue record for this book is available from the British Library.
ISBN 0-85170-554-8

Contents

For Helen

Acknowledgments

For their diverse forms of assistance, I thank: Stuart Kaminsky, Jonathan Rosenbaum, Bill Krohn, Kent Jones, Christopher Frayling, Rob White, Ed Buscombe, Noel King, Helen Bandis, Meaghan Morris, Jenny Darling, Anna Dzenis, and the Research and Information Library of the Australian Film Institute. I also thank Philip Brophy and Lino Caputo for encouraging me to publish my initial thoughts on *Once Upon a Time in America* in a 1987 issue of *Stuffing* magazine. Stills are from BFI Stills, Posters and Designs.

1 Once Upon a Time, Leone

I never thought much about becoming a part of the history of cinema.

Sergio Leone, 1982[1]

Death has a knack of turning the final work of an artist into his or her 'testament' – simultaneously the summation and apotheosis of everything that preceded it. *Once Upon a Time in America* (1983) was a movie that Sergio Leone spent some sixteen years of his life developing, and the only one he completed after *Giu la Testa* in 1971. For admirers of the director it has a special, trembling place in his oeuvre – all the more poignant in that death happens to be one of its central themes.

Once Upon a Time in America tells the epic story of four Jewish gangsters – Noodles (Robert De Niro), Max (James Woods), Patsy (James Hayden) and Cockeye (William Forsythe). Beginning as childhood friends in a squalid district of New York in 1922, they rapidly learn the rules of the street. By 1933 and the end of Prohibition, they have become reasonably glamorous criminals with their own speakeasy, and a secure power network. However, the gang's growing involvement with Jimmy (Treat Williams) and the corrupt union movement slowly drives a wedge between the idealistic Noodles and his more ruthless 'soul brother' Max. Noodles decides to betray the increasingly megalomaniacal Max to the police on the eve of a potentially suicidal Federal Bank robbery – and later sees what appears to be the evidence of all three of his friends murdered in the street.

Stricken with guilt and grief, Noodles decides to exile himself from New York for good – pausing only to claim for himself the gang's reserve of money stashed since childhood, which he finds mysteriously missing. Over thirty years later, in the 1960s, Noodles as an old man is summoned back to his home city. He follows an enigmatic series of commands and clues which lead him eventually to the realisation that Max is still alive – that he had faked his death in 1934 in order to resurrect himself as Bailey, a politician now deeply implicated in the criminal world. Finally, called to Bailey's mansion, Noodles is beseeched by Max to kill him. When Noodles refuses and leaves, Max appears to kill himself by stepping into the back of a garbage truck.

There are many more characters, episodes and tangents in the plot – most significantly, Noodles' disastrous adult relationship with his childhood sweetheart Deborah (Elizabeth McGovern) – and they will be unravelled in the course of this book. The content of the film is inextricably bound up with its peculiar narrative form: a scattered chronology with two framing devices. The bulk of the film is presented in the form of large-scale flashbacks cued by moments in old Noodles' journey in 1968: a long childhood section set in the 20s, and then two sections devoted to the 30s. The 1968 thread is itself framed by scenes from 1934, centred on Noodles' visit to an opium den.

What kind of film is this? Leone is often – and with some justice – circumscribed within a particular global tradition within cinema history. This lineage has attracted many kinds of descriptions and labels: mannerist, baroque, spectacular, exhibitionist, performative, carnivalesque, camp, cartoonish, 'pop formalist' – a cinema of 'effects' rather than meanings, of playful excess rather than classical expressivity. Whatever we choose to call the artistic impulse, there can be no doubt that Leone, beginning with *A Fistful of Dollars* (*Per un pugno di dollari*) in

Little gangsters making a money pact

1964, galvanised this tradition for the modern era more than any other single film-maker.

Bill Krohn has remarked upon the 'tone of defensiveness and grudging approval' evident in even the best scholarly studies since the 60s of Sergio Leone's oeuvre – a defensiveness 'where euphoria and liberating laughter would seem more appropriate'.[2] Why should there be this note of equivocation or special pleading in relation to the critical valuation of Leone? The palpable material thrill, the 'exhilaration of the artist in his own invention'[3] we experience watching his movies is often described as something pure – as 'pure film', or pure cinema. Yet the purity tag can be a curse in film culture, a backhanded compliment which hides a dourer evaluation. Literary standards of artistic worth die hard in most 'educated' cultures; a film that is all style and little content, all surface and no depth, risks being cast out politely as trivial, or of minor significance at best.

Once Upon a Time in America has been celebrated, perhaps more so than any of Leone's previous films, as an example of pure cinema, pure style. Chris Peachment's review in *Sight and Sound*, for example, ends with just such a cinephiliac epiphany: noting the 'memory of an opium-tinted smile at the shadows of puppets on a wall' with which the

Cockeye, Max and Patsy celebrate good times

film leaves its sad hero, Peachment concludes: 'It's not a new observation, but cinema is no more than this.'[4]

Yet *Once Upon a Time in America*, finally, does not sit so easily within such a purist context. The film is a special case within the director's oeuvre. It is obviously still exhibitionistic and operatic like all of Leone's previous work, yet it is not as purely comic book-like as the Westerns. Rather, the more traditional material in *Once Upon a Time in America* – grand themes of literary inspiration, complex emotional structures related to the characters, careful patterning of image and sound motifs, a true 'art film' structure – brought to the fore a side of Leone's cinema that continues to be often obscured or misrecognised. Krohn helps spell out the true lesson: 'After *Once Upon a Time in America* ... there were no grounds for misunderstanding: with the death of Sergio Leone the cinema has lost one of its great Romantic poets.'[5]

However, to argue that, with *Once Upon a Time in America*, Leone got beyond an obsession with pure film and made a perfectly 'organic' work would also constitute a defensive betrayal of Leone, and of his true place in cinema history. I think we must see this film, and Leone's career as a whole, as existing in an impure space where different artistic impulses and cultural traditions interlace. Leone is ultimately not a practitioner of pure cinema, in my view, but rather a richly *impure*, hybrid cinema. And there is no film of his more impure in its concoction of drives and elements than *Once Upon a Time in America*.

The very title of the film announces and prefigures its unusual mixture of moods and styles. Once upon a time: Leone often referred to the film as a 'fairy tale for adults';[6] oneiric, unreal, almost magical elements fill the work. But this fairy tale is collided, contradicted, grounded in a brutal historical reality: in America. For Leone, the fairy tale dimension was essentially cinematic in its substance and its references; time and again he emphasised in interviews and articles that his film could well have been titled 'once upon a time there was a certain kind of cinema'.[7]

So the stake in this tale is a grand, romantic memory of cinema – a lost, classical, generic cinema which forms a mythic 'world apart', marvellous and sufficient unto itself. And of course this cinema, for Leone as for many of us, is essentially American in origin. Just as Leone had previously recreated for himself, in his own feverish way, the mythic world of American Westerns, now he turned to the gangster genre. And, once again – this is the surest sign of Leone's modernity, even his nascent post-modernity – he abstracted the memory of this genre, minimising its conventional plot logic and maximising its 'attractions', its purely spectacular elements.

In Leone's hands, the classic genres become not only Pop Art friezes of iconographic signs and indices, but also a ritual procession of dramatic or 'scenographic' highpoints: 'clinches', charged looks and gestures, moments of recognition. 'Neither a revival nor a disfiguring of the model of reference', writes Michel Sineux, but a 'ritual choreography' returning us to the 'very origins of spectacle' in a primal 'game of masks'.[8] It was as if, for Leone, such disembodied 'quotations' – if they could be made to retain their mythic intensity and potency – might provide a kind of catharsis or ecstasy for modern-day cinephiles pining over their precious 'lost object'. That is why, finally, form can never be 'pure' in Leone's work: at stake in it is a psychic investment, a whole elaborate machine of selfhood, culture and longing …

But, although misty evocations of a golden age loom – the cinema's golden age as much as the characters' carefree, lawless youth – it would be wrong to consider *Once Upon a Time in America* an exercise in nostalgia. There is a wrenching duality in the film: towards epic enchantment on the one hand, and massive disenchantment on the other; the imaginary, movie-made America pitted against the real, historical America. The great 'cinema machine' – and all it means for us as cinephiles – is revved up, but the ultimate destination of this euphoric mental voyage is an extremely black one. Indeed, a melancholic disillusionment is the key emotional note of Leone's testament.

(Overleaf) Old Noodles seemingly back from the dead

2 A Dream and a Map

It has always been one of the special pleasures of movies that they dream worlds and map them at the same time.

Richard Jameson, 1990[9]

The first, bold movement of *Once Upon a Time in America* maps the world of the film – its co-ordinates of time and space, its web of character intrigues – in a gradual, tantalising, poetically allusive way. An aura of enigma hangs over this section like a thick fog. The extreme and quite confronting strangeness of the introduction – certainly the most overt deployment of classic European art cinema devices and mannerisms in Leone's career – undoubtedly exacerbated its distribution troubles in America (outlined in Chapter 8).

One of the most strongly showbiz or 'performative' elements of Leone's approach to cinema is his very theatrical sense of how to introduce the key elements of a film's 'matrix'. This extends not only to the characters – whose stage entrances are always striking and memorable – but also to stylistic elements, such as dialogue, music, even light itself. Once Leone has painstakingly orchestrated the initial appearance of an element, he then sets to combining and interweaving it with the other elements in the ensemble.

There is almost a minute of silence under the opening credits before the first sound appears – diegetic sound of barely distinct revellers, and a performance, over a radio, by Kate Smith of the song 'God Bless America'. This background track continues, almost imperceptibly, throughout the first scene. As the credits draw to a close, other sounds, more distinct and exaggerated, are mixed in; the effect is like listening to a radio play in the dark of the movie theatre. We hear approaching footsteps, and a key opening a door.

The blackness surrounding the credits becomes the darkness of the first image. There is a room, but no lights are on; indistinct objects glisten, and a body moves slowly through the space. It is only in the fifth shot that a lamplight reveals the full facial features of Eve (Darlanne

Fleugel). As she fiddles with the lamp switch, signs of disturbance and menace immediately fill her consciousness. The hoods who lurk in the dark are showmen no less than Leone himself, and they announce their presence through extravagant, spectacular signs: the first is the bullet-ridden outline of a body in the bed that Eve shares, presumably, with her lover. Already, even to show us simple gestures like Eve's prowl through the darkness or her pulling back of the bedsheet, Leone's camera is craning and tracking with great, elegant sweeps.

The second sign of the gangsters' presence is more immediately shocking: the butt of a gun smashes the glass framing a picture of a man, Noodles (thus allowing us a first, fleeting, indirect glimpse of the film's hero, and of Robert De Niro). Now it is time for the kind of exhibitionistic introduction of bad guys that Leone did so often in his Westerns – a trick of staging that film editors call a 'reveal', and which Leone used more consistently and lovingly than perhaps any director in the history of world cinema. The camera moves up the arm of a man to reveal his ugly, solemn puss in close-up; a second hood moves from darkness into a pool of light, in mid-shot; a third moves into a wide-shot grouping with his pals. The progression is hierarchical and musical; it's also perfectly generic, and even a little corny in a deliberate, affectionate way. It sets up the kind of pulp poetry that is to characterise this film from start to end.

Now, almost three minutes into the film, comes its first line of dialogue, from the chief hood: 'Where is he? Where is he hiding?' This sets the mode for all the film's dialogue – terse, staccato, epigrammatic, working the vein of either a hard-boiled lyricism or an oblique intimation of unsavoury truths. The dialogue in this first scene, and the scene that follows with Moe (Larry Rapp), also drops hints about the narrative intrigue to be unfolded: Noodles is a 'stoolie who rats on his own friends'.

Eve is brutally, coldly murdered, and the third hood is told to wait there in the apartment. Leone cuts suddenly to a gruesome close-up of a bloody Moe, strung up and being beaten. The scene is a slight, transitional one, but begins the mapping of a crucial, elaborate,

Eve faces death; a hierarchy of henchmen; Moe menaced and humiliated

Public image: Noodles reads all about it; Noodles hidden by the crowd; the charred and unrecognisable body.

constantly transformed space in the film – the various rooms and zones of Moe's restaurant. Thanks to Carlo Simi's precise, intricate art direction, this is one of the key 'sites' of the film which retains enough of a recognisable, physical identity in each of its successive incarnations to reveal, or cast into relief, the changes wrought by time and history.

So far, Leone has been easing us into the film – an opening flurry of sights, sounds and enigmas where, as Godard once said of his film *Passion* (1982), 'it's the beginning of the movie and your foot is not yet inside your shoe'.[10] The third scene is immediately more textured and intense. Here the vast, multi-level space of an opium den is intensely mapped in a relay of gestures, movements and looks. An old, stiff Chinese woman enters the frame; behind her in the distance is a dance of shadow puppets, and around her is the soft flurry of gongs. (Tony Rayns notes that the shadow-play derives from Indonesian theatre, a version of the creation myth known as the *Ramayana*.)[11] Immediately picking up her motion, the camera tracks with her down a passageway. She stops and looks up at a man who understands her signal and proceeds to open a door behind him. Doors have an ubiquitous, insistent presence in this film, transformed from functional objects into poetic markers of passage.

The camera tracks back with this second Chinese figure and uses the path of his ritual movements to reveal to us a new, more secret, more sumptuous space in the den. A brief montage knits together a panorama of views: bodies variously naked, languid, asleep, young and old, American and Asian. Only in the fourth shot does the man kneel down to reveal Noodles, supine. His eyes are closed, he seems barely conscious. The Chinaman makes Noodles drink something, and after a few moments he chokes on it, jolts his head up, and grabs for a newspaper. A pan follows Noodles' gaze to the latest piece of plot information on that front page: the faces of three men, and a headline, 'Bootleggers Trapped by Feds; Three Slain'. Noodles' head goes back down to the pillow, and his eyes close again.

Now a phone rings. It is a grating, harsh, loud ring, and it shocks Noodles. He casts around; there is no phone anywhere in sight. His assistant placates him with a long opium pipe, and Noodles sucks on it frantically, desperately. Finally, as he receives a leg massage, the opium appears to kick in; the muscles on his face relax into a dumb, inscrutable mass. Leone's camera pans across to a lamp flame, out of focus, which provides the visual-graphic transition to another obscure light source. This turns out to be a street light, slightly swinging in the rain.

All throughout these last few gestures and images, the phone has just kept on ringing, with no fading down in volume. It will ring, in all, twenty-four times, for over three and a half minutes. Just when you think this phone has stopped its hellish cry, you realise that Leone has only teased us by fractionally lengthening the pause between rings. Now the phone becomes the aural trigger for a cascade of shots, fragmentary glimpses of some larger flashback, as incomprehensible and as tantalising as a movie trailer – an instance of that 'ritual choreography' in action. The first, rain-swept tableau is clear enough: photographers darting about, three dead bodies being laid out, zipped into bags and labelled. We observe the inscription of their official names – Patrick Goldberg, Philip Stein, Maximilian Bercovicz – and we note their Jewishness (soon we will come to know them by their everyday names: Patsy, Cockeye and Max). We see two of the faces clearly, but the third is a charcoal-blackened, unrecognisable horror – an important plot clue for later. And, between these glimpses, we have (courtesy of Leone and his cinematographer Tonino Delli Colli) our first really arresting portrait-study of De Niro as the adult Noodles, as he moves into position and the zoom lens tightens its gaze on him: head slightly cocked, only the right side of the face illuminated, troubled and secretive eyes, a street light behind him.

A sudden darkness, gradually illuminated first by candles and then a glaring spotlight: a coffin, representing the Prohibition era, is being carried into a room of anonymous revellers as mock-mournful traditional jazz plays. Now the images become more disorienting, cutting faster and with less explication: Max, Patsy and Cockeye gesture to someone off-screen; a woman (Tuesday Weld) looks anxiously in that same direction; we catch Noodles in the act of kissing an apparently troubled Eve on the neck. A Leonesque 'mapping' shot follows: Noodles traverses the space of the room in order to exit through a door, and the camera zooms back to show the whole scene. Max looks off-screen again, very intensely.

The camera tracks into a phone, and we hear yet another maddening ring. Is this the source of our, and Noodles', aural anguish? Something surreal and magical then occurs: Noodles picks up the phone, but the ringing sound continues. Noodles dials a number; the camera flicks nervously along his arm to his face. Here's another phone, with a handy name plate beside it: Sgt P. Halloran. Is this the ringing phone? A hand enters the frame and picks it up, but before we can verify our hypothesis another sound, like a screeching feedback wail, begins – and cutting now back to Noodles in the opium den, we see that the sound is going through his head like a knife. The phone sound has been interrupted, cast into abeyance as a poetic mystery. What was it, where was it? Presumably it was something playing itself out in Noodles' head, but what exactly prompted this auditory hallucination? Doubtless a wake-up call, a call to remember – but from whom?

Once Upon a Time in America has already, in this first movement, set up its key, driving, narrative enigma. It is a mystery of 'agency', one common to many noirish plots: Noodles is a puppet-hero, and someone is behind the scenes pulling the strings. The film has also begun mapping its key spatial and temporal co-ordinates. It does so in an intricate, even obsessive manner: forever spiralling back, returning to certain sites, scenes and gestures, and thus investing them with a charged emotion, a pregnant significance, and what Raymond Bellour calls a 'textual volume'.[12]

The essential principle of Leonesque *mise en scène* – whether in its wildest, most expressionistic and cartoonish moments, or its quietest, most subtle ones – is the poetic interrelation of the cinematic functions of time and space. Of course, this could be routinely said of many film-makers. But few have gone as far as Leone in marrying the audience's sense of dramaturgical space – the tensions and possibilities instantly conjured by the respective positions of people and objects – to its enforced experience of screen duration. As Vincent Ostria has put it, for

Leone 'time is a means for exaggerating the density and intensity of space'[13] – as in the scene, reminiscent in its outrageousness of the elaborate clinches that fill Leone's Westerns, in which Noodles gradually draws and rivets everyone's attention at a tense gang meeting by stirring his coffee with a spoon. And the vice versa of Ostria's comment is also surely the case: the seeming vastness and cold immutability of the funereal spaces in *Once Upon a Time in America* intensify the melancholy of passing time.

In the opening scenes, it is the territorial movements of the hoods, and the scrambled mental flashback of Noodles, which allow the effect and structure of textual reconnaissance across time and space, the 'sumptuous … and baroque'[14] work of 'memory spectacle' for the viewer.[15] But soon enough Leone will assume much more directly – in an open display of his art-film mastery – the responsibility for these kinds of shuttlings and mappings across time, space and events. From the image of Noodles in 1933 approaching the mural-decorated train gate – after he has booked a ticket to 'anywhere, the first bus … one way', a truly hard-boiled destination – the film cuts to a mirror at that same site, thirty-five years later. And into the frame of that mirror steps a shockingly old Noodles. Of the Beatles classic that Morricone here pillages for his score, only two words are sung: 'Yesterday … Suddenly'. And Noodles, clearly, isn't half the man he used to be.

3 The Mummy's Curse

The story of these Jewish gangsters ... attached itself to me like the malediction of the Mummy in the old movie with Boris Karloff.

Sergio Leone, 1984[16]

Once Upon a Time in America began to develop in Leone's mind even before *Once Upon a Time in the West*. He envisaged, at that time, a loose 'American trilogy' covering the founding of the West, the Mexican revolution (*Giu la testa*) and finally the gangster milieu of the 20s. As early as 1970, Leone worked with Norman Mailer on a script for *Once Upon a Time in America*; shortly after, he turned down the offer to direct another gangster epic, *The Godfather* (1972).

Leone's development continued steadily for the next decade; beyond the script itself, he immersed himself in painstaking historical research. His passion for the project spilled over into his interim work as producer. There is only an abrupt black screen on current video copies of the flamboyant Terence Hill comedy-Western *My Name is Nobody* (1973) – produced, 'based on an idea' and partly directed by Leone – to testify to what I clearly remember from my teenage viewing of the film: the written announcement that Hill's adventures would be continued in the forthcoming *Once Upon a Time in America*!

Then Leone went to America in the hope of setting up the project. He did not always envisage that he would direct it; among others, Peter Bogdanovich and Milos Forman were interviewed for this position. Throughout the 70s, Leone worked on the script with many different writers. The initial, guiding conception was very different from the one he eventually settled on. The crime novelist Pete Hamill (himself interviewed as a prospective scriptwriter) recalls Leone's excited verbal description, 'one morning in the early 70s', of how the film would begin: 'We open at the bottom of the harbour of New York. Right at the bottom! Then a body comes down, floating down. ... The body comes down, down, down. And then: close-up. Big, big close-up. A green eye!'[17]

We have one indication on film of this original script conception. In the early 70s, Leone worked with the American screenwriter Robert Dillon on a draft. According to Leone, Dillon subsequently adapted part of this material (including the opening scene) for the script of John Frankenheimer's *99 and 44/100% Dead* (1974).[18] This curiously hip, sardonic, Pop Art gangster film is in many respects close to the stylistic mannerisms of Leone's Westerns – right down to its exaggerated gun-shot sounds and the iconic casting of a gaunt, chiselled Chuck Connors – but it has none of the sombreness of the gangster epic that Leone would eventually make.

After Frankenheimer's film appeared, Leone resolved to transform the central idea of *Once Upon a Time in America*. Over time he enlisted six writers for the task. Five are credited in the film, beside Leone himself: Enrico Medioli (who worked on many Visconti films including *Rocco and His Brothers*, which prefigures Leone's film in several respects); the duo of Leonardo Benvenuti and Piero De Bernardi (active since the mid-50s and known as the 'the most prolific writing team in Italy'); ex-critic Franco Ferrini, who edited a special issue of the magazine *Bianco e nero* on Leone in 1971; and Franco 'Kim' Arcalli, a co-writer and editor for Bertolucci, who died in 1978, four years before shooting began.[19] Intensive revision of the drafts arrived at during the latter half of the 70s – when 'each successive screenplay came out inferior to the concept', in Leone's recollection[20] – began in 1981. Now the director, after interviewing many American writers, called upon the services of Stuart Kaminsky, a noted cinema scholar who had written several appreciative articles on Leone's work, and a prolific novelist and biographer.

By this advanced stage of the scripting process, some of the credited writers had no involvement in the extensive re-drafting. In 1984, Leone unambiguously cited Kaminsky and Benvenuti as the principal contributors who 'miraculously concluded' the screenplay.[21] Due to contractual complications arising from the Ladd Company's re-editing of the finished film, Kaminsky is credited solely with 'additional dialogue', but he in fact crafted all of the film's dialogue. According to

Kaminsky's account, Benvenuti was primarily responsible for devising the physical, visual action of scenes, while Medioli's principal contribution to the collective scripting process at this advanced stage was 'to insure that we remembered the epic nature of the film to be shot'.

A world apart: the decadent opium den

Kaminsky – who also spent several weeks working specifically with De Niro – regards his major creative contribution as 'turning the characters [i.e. Noodles and Max] into distinct individuals representing opposite ends of a spectrum'.[22]

At the very origin of the project lay an autobiographical book published in America in 1952, *The Hoods* by 'Harry Grey' (pseudonym for David Aaronson), which Leone stumbled upon in the late 60s.[23] Leone and his scriptwriters added much to the material in the book. Grey's narrative (which is arranged in conventional, linear chronology) ends in the 1930s exactly where the film begins – with Noodles in the opium den, wracked with grief, about to make his escape from New York. But most of the key characters – Noodles, Max, Patsy, Cockeye, Dominic, Moe, Peggy, Eve, Deborah (named Dolores in the book) come from Grey, as well as a number of crucial elements (Noodles' escapist use of opium; Deborah's showbiz career; Max's megalomania) and specific scenes (Noodles' toilet exchange with Peggy; his troubled date with Deborah; the jewellery heist that introduces Carol, who is named Betty in the book). From the vast amount of material in the novel that Leone either discarded or simplified, one strand is particularly striking: Noodles is so nicknamed in the book because he is a thinker – he constantly reads authors such as Freud, and dreams of the day when he will himself be a writer.

Leone described *The Hoods* as 'a perfect and loving hymn to the cinema', but in a peculiar way. 'Grey told me he had written his book against Hollywood, while he was imprisoned in Sing Sing. But, on the contrary, his book resembled a voice-over by a bad Hollywood screenwriter.' Leone was intrigued, above all, by the manner in which generic 'citations, allusions, adventures and even psychological considerations' had unconsciously entered and shaped Grey's account of his own life.[24]

Actually obtaining, and then keeping, the rights to the book led Leone down a long and tortuous path. Initially, in the late 60s, Embassy Pictures in America already had an option on it. This was then passed on to the director Dan Curtis, who refused to make a deal with Leone and Gérard Lebovici's French company Génovès. By the mid-70s Leone had hooked up with Italian producer Alberto Grimaldi, who cleverly proposed to finance another project for Curtis (the horror film *Burnt Offerings*, 1976) in exchange for rights to *The Hoods*. 'That was already the first sign of where things were heading,' Leone later ruefully commented[25] – for then the project stalled for three or four years with Grimaldi, who struggled with losses incurred by his big-budget productions *Il Casanova di Federico Fellini* (1976) and Bertolucci's *Novecento* (1977). Eventually, Leone joined forces with producer Arnon Milchan (*King of Comedy*, *Six Degrees of Separation*), who sued Grimaldi in order to regain the elusive rights. And of course Leone had further legal problems ahead, after the film's completion, with Milchan and the Ladd Company.

Pre-production casting was extremely extensive – 3,000 actors interviewed for 110 speaking roles, and 500 auditions videotaped. De Niro had been approached much earlier, during the making of *The Godfather, Part II* (1974), and Leone offered him the choice of playing either lead. Actors considered for the role of Max included Jon Voight, William Hurt, Joe Pesci, Harvey Keitel and John Malkovich. Liza Minnelli and Geena Davis auditioned for the part of Deborah; Leone got the idea of casting Elizabeth McGovern from Milos Forman's *Ragtime* (1981). Clint Eastwood turned down the part of an Irish

Child and adult: Noodles, Deborah, Max

gangster (presumably the character of Jimmy O'Donnell which went to Treat Williams).

The shooting of *Once Upon a Time in America*, covering seven months in 1982, was complex and expensive; *Variety* estimated its final budget at over $30 million. The central street set of the film was created on an actual Brooklyn street, and then built twice over in Rome and in Montreal. The interiors and exteriors of certain key places (such as Moe's bar) were shot on different continents. Various locations in America – a beach near Miami, landscapes in New Jersey – were knit and matched with locations in Europe, such as the Excelsior Hotel in Venice, where Noodles and Deborah dine. The opium den was constructed at Cinecittà.

At several points during the planning of the film, Leone's collaborators raised the matter of the material's Jewish origins and elements. It is true that Leone's extensive research on the Jewish-American milieu of his characters really boiled down to a brief show of 'local colour' early on (particularly in the panoramic street scenes). A great deal of specific ethnic detail in dialogue references, behaviour and setting was excised by Leone from successive drafts of the script. He vetoed the idea of having the main characters speak Yiddish to each

Max and Noodles in New York's Jewish district

other with English sub-titles. David Thomson may have committed to print the casual musing of many viewers when he wrote of *Once Upon a Time in America*: 'Its would-be Jewish gangsters seemed very Italian.'[26] And who can blame him? When it was suggested to Leone, repeatedly, that he should cast some Jewish actors in the film, he is rumoured to have replied: 'Jews, Italians, there is no difference.'

4 A Pulp Fiction

The fact is, I've always made epic films and the epic, by definition, is a masculine universe.

Sergio Leone, 1984[27]

In many reviews, whether positive or negative, written at the moment of the release of *Once Upon a Time in America*, there are troubled references to the film's pulp elements – or, more exactly, to the contradiction between these elements and Leone's obvious aspiration to make an art film. Michel Chion, for instance, lamented its 'somewhat dubious' touches of 'comic book sadism'.[28] Meaghan Morris argued the toss differently; for her it was properly a 'pulp film saved only by its splendid flourishes of violence from its fate as mere failed art'.[29] The most damning judgment came from Brian Case, for whom the project's 'pulp origins' in Grey's *The Hoods* were 'all too apparent', and in the event unable to sustain the 'reverberating chasms of tragedy upon which Leone insists'.[30]

There is no doubt that the most shocking impurity of Leone's film is precisely its shameless mixture of sublimity and pulp, the sacred and the profane. This is partly a result of Leone's unique position and intervention in cinema history. As an artist looking around and flexing his muscles in the early 60s, Leone was instantly an odd, potent, combustible mixture of impulses. He was drawn, on the one hand, to the ruptures of tone, the violent contrasts of mood that characterise, for example, the modernist narratives of Renoir, Truffaut or (later) Scorsese, with their paradoxical, dynamic equilibrium of parts. On the other hand, Leone was equally drawn (like many modernists) to the energy and *élan* of popular forms and genres. Leone embraced the truly 'plebian' depths of popular culture – his own, Italian popular culture as much as the 'exotic', romantic American culture he cultivated as a fan. That led him, quite naturally, to vulgarity, farce, low sexual humour and 'comic book sadism'. It was a sensibility that stirred – and can still stir today – an inevitable *frisson* in respectable film cultures.

In Leone's cinema the gender and character of pulp fiction are essentially, even overwhelmingly masculine. In a book of interviews conducted by Noël Simsolo, Leone remarked that *Once Upon a Time in America* encapsulated his 'definitive phantasms: my relation to America, lost friendship, and the cinema'.[31] When Leone refers to friendship, he of course means the fraught friendship between men. Elsewhere, he elaborated: 'Virile friendship is one of the dominant themes of all my films. It is probably the only feeling which perseveres, still today, and which expresses, as far as I am concerned, the harmonious synthesis of man and his moral vicissitudes.'[32]

Is virile friendship, however unconsciously on Leone's part, a coded phrase for homo-eroticism? The film replays, on a grand scale, the typical buddy adventures in which we routinely recognise, these days, the love that dare not speak its name: guys who go robbing and fighting, drinking and whoring together, whose sexual lives centre on the same woman, and whose greatest, most serious emotional bond is ultimately with each other. There are typically vulgar indices of such homo-eroticism throughout the 1920s and 30s segments of the film: the gang members regularly joke about taking or giving it 'up the ass', and when Carol mistakes Max's penis for Noodles' in the back room of Moe's Prohibition-era nightclub, the latter remarks, 'we been hangin' out so long together we're startin' to look alike.'

What is undeniable is that the rituals of male bonding between these gangsters – including all their dealings in violence – are utterly sexualised. The phallic character of the film's violent mayhem is insisted upon by Leone from its first moments. Eve is shot in the chest; Moe has a gun shaft inserted into his mouth; a hood sadistically toys with an anonymous prostitute in the opium den by grazing her bare nipple with his gun. Such details carry a chilling air, but they sit on the same continuum as the spirited, anarchic gestures of male comedy that fill the film.

The brutish vulgarity of men was something Leone celebrated: it provided the occasion for a raucous comedy influenced, variously, by James Cagney's gangster exploits, by Chaplin at his least inhibited, and

by Fellini's wild boy gangs in *I vitelloni* (1953) and *Amarcord* (1973). Our first glimpse of the young gang in action shows what at first seems to be the lot of them gaily pissing onto a news-stand; a slight camera shift then reveals they are spraying from oil cans hidden inside their coats. Later, the hilarious scene of baby-switching in a hospital is an unambiguous celebration of the gang's power to 'castrate' its enemies –

'Startin' to look alike': Carol fondles the masked men; phallic exuberance – setting fire to the news-stand

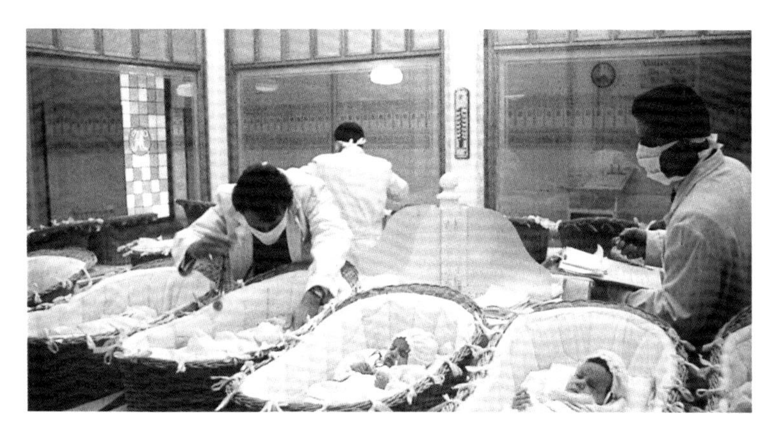

as evidenced in the horror of the police chief (Danny Aiello) when he discovers his baby no longer has a penis – and to upturn the social order (Max: 'We're better than fate. We give some the good life, we give it to others right up the ass!'). The equally outrageous scene of the jewel store robbery – in which Carol urges Noodles to beat her and 'make it look real' – makes a number of viewers and commentators wonder exactly when high-spirited, phallic humour shades into full-blown sexual abuse in Leone's tough-guy universe.

But we do not have to peg Leone as either a closet queer or a raging misogynist in order to grasp that male friendship was, for him, an intense and privileged arena of human relationships – a tragic arena in which the deepest love was at stake. *Once Upon a Time in America* ultimately raises the emotional intensity that flows between men from a jokey, vulgar plane to a more sublime, sentimental, even romantic plateau. It is hard not to view Noodles' behaviour as ardent when, as a young teenager (played by Scott Tiler), he panics at the thought that Max (Rusty Jacobs) has just drowned in the river. It is equally hard not to view old Max's behaviour in the penultimate scene, as he pleads with Noodles to take his rightful revenge, as that of a desperate, spurned lover.

The film dramatises a two-way male dependency; for Tony Rayns, the 'relationship between Noodles and Max – grounded, crucially, in a

Castrating power: the hospital baby-switch

shared memory – is finally a heart-breaking story of mutual need'.[33] In a 30s scene, Carol in fact makes the romantic logic of the relationship between these two men matter-of-factly explicit. She suggests to Noodles, with no apparent derision, that he put himself in prison along with Max, 'if you can't bear to be without him'. And Max, too, gets extremely close to acknowledging this logic when he reminds Noodles in 1968: 'Your eyes were too full of tears to see that it wasn't me lying there burnt up on the street.'

But there is one absolutely primary dark side in the mythic scenario of virile friendship. And that is the recognition that, inherent within such an intense male bond, underwriting all its glory, there is a profound and devastating capacity for betrayal. It is from Max's central act of betrayal that the moral vicissitudes of the plot and the whole dank mood of the film – its guilt-ridden, half-life ambience – are generated.

Max the trickster manipulates an ardent Noodles

5 Gangster Without Glory

I think it might be a pity ... to abandon completely something that was so exciting in the traditional cinema: this play with the protagonist, the so-called central character, the Hitchcockian-Langian play on the phony central consciousness and all that this allows.

Jacques Rivette, 1973[34]

Once Upon a Time in America is sometimes discussed or presented – particularly by its home-video packaging – as a gangster movie. Yet, taken within this genre, it is surely a very curious and attenuated exercise. The classically wild, euphoric moments of a gangster's escapades – the heists, shoot-outs, daring clinches with cops or rival mobsters – are few and far between, and a number of them, such as the 'payback' murder of Crowning (Gerard Murphy) are the most perfunctory and forgettable passages of the movie. One particular scene – Noodles entering a feather cleaning plant alone to hunt down and kill the last member of a rival gang – indicates most clearly the film's deflationary tone. In a John Woo movie, such a set-up would provide the occasion for a galvanising, kinetic showdown, a climactic, face-to-face combat of warriors. In Leone's rendering, the scene downplays action and excitement, relying almost entirely on a haunted, ghostly atmosphere and texture more akin to Dreyer's *Vampyr* (1932) than the average criminal saga. Leone was eloquent about what, in this respect, most attracted to him to Grey's novel: precisely the premise it offered of a 'gangster story without glory'.[35]

It is unsurprising that many commentators on the film are moved to invoke Robert Warshow and his justly classic, seminal essay of 1948, 'The Gangster as Tragic Hero'.[36] Warshow stresses the gleefully arrested development of the genre's hero figures, whose behaviour 'appeals most to adolescents'.[37] And Leone's film at least fulfils this contract of the genre: the fleeting moments of euphoria that Leone allows his two-bit gangsters are almost purely of a boyish, childlike nature. The exchange of children in the hospital (set to the accompaniment of Rossini's 'The

Thieving Magpie') is the prime instance of this, right down to the image of Cockeye drinking gaily from a baby's bottle. From the 20s to the 30s, these gangsters just never grow up.

But, in the course of this story, two members of the gang will die ignominiously, off-screen, and the other two will live to old age – neither destiny a fitting one for gangsters who should go out in a blaze of glory. Even the slow-motion death of gang member Dominic (Noah Moazezi)

A haunted ghostly clinch: Noodles among the feathers; 'I slipped': Dominic's death

in childhood, felled by a bullet in the street, suggests less a sense of grandeur than of waste, confusion, a twist of destiny both painful and incomprehensible to those left behind, particularly to Noodles who dwells until adulthood (in his exchange with Deborah on the beach) on Dominic's odd, last words: 'I slipped.'

So, what strange kind of gangster movie is *Once Upon a Time in America*? Morris gives its 'sprawling' story an intriguing context: 'It is a type of narrative which almost forms a genre in itself as a broken-down version of the nineteenth-century novel-saga of social and personal genesis.'[38] In literary terms, this loose genre takes us back to lofty authors who were touchstones for Leone when conceiving the film, such as William Faulkner and John Dos Passos. Today, as Morris notes, the genre is mainly practised by writers of 'high-class potboilers', such as William Styron, John Fowles and E.L. Doctorow – contemporaries whose work has interesting affinities with Leone's.

'Social and personal genesis' implies a certain epic consistency and linearity – a hero who grows from auspicious origins into destined manhood. At the centre of such an action epic there has to be a hero who sees and hears and smells all, who traverses and orders physical space, whose smallest signals register as commands that result in decisive actions – for example, the 'Mr Big' so beloved of gangster mythology and fantasy, from Cagney to Harry Belafonte in Altman's *Kansas City* (1996).

But *Once Upon a Time in America* is not an epic of manifest destiny, like Gance's *Napoleon* (1927) or Mel Gibson's *Braveheart* (1995). It is a film of breakdown and crack-up, of loss and oblivion. Its form resembles a shattered, scattered epic. Contemporary gangster films embody and dramatise, with particular force, the 'crisis of the action-image' that Gilles Deleuze broadly attributes to international cinema in the wake of World War II.[39] According to his account, the ritual, ceremonial actions that once happily cohered externally oriented, highly physical forms like the Western, the war movie and the gangster film – actions like hauling a wagon train across the landscape or having a shoot-out – suddenly slow down, become complicated, and often get blocked long before the usual point of completion or fulfilment. Heroes (such as

John Wayne in *The Searchers*, James Stewart in Anthony Mann's films and *Rear Window*) become disturbed, obsessive, frustrated, sometimes literally immobile figures, caught in vain patterns of desperate repetition, barred from the very scenes or stages where they once would have taken such decisive action. And, most importantly, what seemed to be the driving, motor force of these narratives – the hero's own subjectivity, his will and his gaze – is suddenly, rudely ejected from a sovereign seat of power.

Betrayal – especially betrayal between brothers, or lifelong buddies – has always been a prime motor of gangster stories.[40] Leone's film superimposes two stories of betrayal, of two very different shades. Noodles betrays Max out of love, out of a desire to save him from himself. Noodles tries to remove Max from the stage of history, but then sees this plan backfire horribly: the grief and pain this error causes him

prompt his own instant and prolonged withdrawal from the world. Of course Noodles does not see, at that moment, what he assumes he sees. He is caught in a frame-up, and in that trap he 'misrecognises' the truth before his very eyes. Like many elegiac mystery stories, Leone's film traces an epic arc from a fundamental moment of blindness to an ultimate act of vision – a vision that finally includes total understanding.[41] It is in part due to this narrative structure that *Once*

The changing times: a party to end prohibition

Upon a Time in America is such a drama of vision – a drama in which so much power and gravity are invested in what characters (especially Noodles) see, and in what Leone 'reveals'.

In his complete and utter act of misrecognition, Noodles becomes a *dupe*. And the story of the dupe is one of the distinguishing motifs of post-war 'crisis cinema', beginning in the days of film noir. From *Mr Arkadin* (Welles, 1955) to *Strange Days* (Bigelow, 1995), male heroes find themselves duped by those closest to them – not merely those least suspected, but those most totally and blindly trusted. This is the larger, more brilliant, and certainly more evil form of betrayal – the betrayal that exploits love, the sweet cheat.

Films in which a central character is duped have, generally speaking, strikingly convoluted or baroque narrative forms. This is because every safe, classical assumption on the part of an innocent viewer – like the assumption that the hero sees and hears all, that he is driving the story, that he is on a straight line heading towards the truth – is thrown completely out of kilter. Suddenly the grandiloquent, reassuring artifice of a certain kind of storytelling is laid bare, and trashed; suddenly, to adopt Rivette's words, the hero is revealed as simply a 'so-called central character', and his subjectivity merely a 'phony central consciousness'. In place of such certainties, we are plunged instead into a universe of malevolent, shadowy forces, of appearances that always lie, of vertiginous traumas and hallucinations born of all-pervasive paranoia – which, cinematically, is rendered in perpetual shifts, inversions and clashes of narrational points-of-view.[42]

In the gangster genre, the theme of betrayal has often found its privileged form in such an eviction: the hero's loss of control over his own story. For Leone this theft of a life is made even more bitter-sweet by the fact that it is stage-managed by the hero's veritable 'double' or doppelgänger – his beloved brother, his mirror, his killer. This doppelgänger motif is worked out in great detail. From the start, Max is cast as the one who dominates and manipulates Noodles' life – the 'mother' who calls him (as Deborah taunts), the one who literally takes his time away from him (in their youthful manoeuvring over a watch). In

a key 20s scene set at the Lower New York Bay, Max disappears under the water and then appears, in order to taunt Noodles with the proof of his own insane trusting love: 'What would you do without me?'

Much later, Max will be the only person with enough power over Noodles to find him and call him back, this time seemingly from the dead. It is a call that he cannot refuse, and the gradual traces of which he obediently follows. And when Noodles reaches this pre-arranged destination, he will encounter Max's own exact double, his son, sitting on a 'throne' as his father has done, from his very first appearance (on the junk wagon), through his gangster days (where he sports a throne that belonged to a seventeenth-century Pope!). In the mythology of the genre, Max represents a new, sophisticated kind of gangster hero, the upwardly mobile operator who can rise above the 'stink of the streets'. What he

'I'm gonna do something with your time': Whitey, Max, Noodles

(top) Max on his throne

does in the Bay, disappearing and reappearing, he will do later in his criminal career on a much larger scale. He is a trickster, a chameleon, able to reinvent himself to ride the waves of history. He has no sentimental attachment to his origins, and no ties that bind him to his intimates.

In the classic inventory of the gangster hero's possessions – the money, the power, the girl as Tony (Al Pacino) orders them in De Palma's *Scarface* (1983) – we have the perfect list of everything which Max systematically takes away from Noodles. And also his very life, which, as a result of Max's primal act of betrayal, becomes an abject, ghostly state of suspended animation. Max says as much: 'I took away your whole life from you. All I left for you was thirty-five years of grief for having killed me.' Yet Leone will have history turn on Max too. As 'Secretary Bailey' surveys the bank of TV monitors recording the crowd at his party, he drily remarks: 'Rats usually desert a sinking ship. In my case, they appear to be flocking on board.' Like another smooth operator, the gangster hero of Budd Boetticher's *The Rise and Fall of Legs Diamond* (1960), Max's escalating ruthlessness has perhaps led him to lose sight of the most essential trick of manipulation in his repertoire of strategies: as Alice (Karen Steele) remarks wisely in Boetticher's film, 'that was the magic – as long as someone loved you, you were OK.'

Time finally runs out for 'Secretary Bailey'

6 A Violent Night

Because he loves as man *only*, not as human being, for this reason there is in his sexual feeling something narrow, seeming wild, spiteful, time-bound, un-eternal.

Rainer Maria Rilke, 'Letters on Love', 1903[43]

Bill Krohn testifies that, on hearing of Leone's death on 30 April 1989, he 'responded to the news, as I'm sure many did, in the most obvious way: I put on Morricone's score for *Once Upon a Time in the West* and listened again to the title track. What beautiful music … .'[44] The album of Morricone's score for *Once Upon a Time in America*, too, has an almost talismanic power and poignancy as a souvenir for lovers of the film. It is certainly more melodic, less radical and atonal, than much of Morricone's screen work – with relatively conventional orchestral arrangements and instrumentation (ocarina and pan flute notwithstanding), and a familiar, easily identifiable distribution of themes for different sections and moods of the movie.

But, in a quiet and subtle way, there are unusual aspects of this score that create complex emotional effects. Like Leone's narrative construction and *mise en scène*, Morricone offers us an intricately and tightly interwoven spread of musical elements. The 'cross-referencing' effects of the music multiply, as the various themes travel through the film in diverse transformations. The jaunty 'Cockeye's Theme', led by the pan flute, is a transposition of 'Once Upon a Time in America' into the key of C major. 'Amapola', the Calle/Gamse standard appropriated by Morricone, appears first as diegetic music emitting from a gramophone, then as orchestral music played in the restaurant (both times in the key of A major), and finally – in a stirring juxtaposition – it is shifted into E major, as it weaves in and out like a faint, decaying echo between the now familiar phrases of 'Deborah's Theme'.

There are three particularly memorable musical themes in *Once Upon a Time in America*: all tend, at various points of the film, towards a mournful, elegiac air. These are the main theme, 'Once Upon a Time in America'; 'Poverty', with its distinctive 'cheap piano' melody; and

'Deborah's Theme'. Morricone seems to have designed these themes so that they can blur together – both during the course of the film and later, in the audience's memory. All three are in the key of E (major and/or minor). All employ an unusually extended, unbroken melodic line (a characteristic of many Morricone scores). And all come to rest, at roughly the same key moment, on the 'hanging' note of D sharp.

It is the relentless, inexorable blurring of the upbeat, action-oriented melodies with the more sentimental 'Deborah's Theme' across the course of the narrative that enables the film as a totality to be located within the subjectivity of its hero. Morricone avowed as much when he commented that his musical themes 'come into the film when the camera looks into the eyes of the character. The theme then singles out what he is thinking at that moment, what is going on inside, what he is about to say. The pain and joy inside a character is what my music is about.'[45]

Yet this blurring of themes and dramatic moods – which occurs every time the score moves in on that ominous D sharp note – also serves to express (in a way that only music entwined with an unfolding narrative can) a certain chasm or abyss. And this is the dissociation, effecting and lacerating Noodles at every step of his journey, between the male sphere of gangsterism and the (conventionally) female sphere of romantic love. In this structure of dissociation, the image of Deborah often appears as a divine respite, the haven in Noodles' heartless, brutal underworld: after suffering a beating from Bugsy (James Russo), after the tawdry, first-hand experiences of sexual dysfunction and blackmail on the rooftop, it is always to Deborah that he flies. And yet, ultimately, this very idealisation merely exaggerates and reinforces the impossible distance between them.[46]

This raises what can justly be described as the relentless determinism of Leone's film. Men and women, winners and losers, the screwers and the screwed ('I'm gettin' screwed up the ass!' is a frequent cry of the young gang members), the beautiful and the ugly, the blessed and the damned: the film marks, over and over, the abyss that separates these terms. All the characters are fixed in their relative positions, and are fools to believe otherwise. There is a savage, almost Darwinian hierarchy to such placement. In one of the most brutal exchanges of the film, Noodles says to Moe on his return to the bar in 1968: 'You can always tell the winners at the starting gate. You can always tell the winners – and you can tell the losers.' Gesturing to Moe, he unkindly amplifies his point: 'Who woulda put a penny on you?' Moe is more generous: 'I woulda put everything I had on you.' But Noodles remains unmoved: 'Yeah, and you woulda lost.'

It is possible to suspect that there is something rigid or contrived, strangely maudlin or overly tortured, in this deterministic logic. It shades easily into fatalism – and doesn't one of those Coney Island posters in the 30s train station advertise a 'Fatalist Supreme'? In cinema, we might associate varying shades of fatalism with Lang or Hitchcock, De Palma or Téchiné – while an opposing, freer, more generously humanist principle is espoused by Jean Renoir or Wayne Wang. But Leone at least

Doorway to a dark future: the train station

invests his deterministic theorem with an unmistakeable intensity – and nowhere more so than in the drama involving Noodles and Deborah.

Their gloomy, morbid romance starts, as everything in this film does, in childhood – in homage, perhaps to Old Hollywood romances such as *Peter Ibbetson* (1935), with their characteristically ecstatic conjoining of innocence and intensity. The first flashback of the elderly Noodles is to a moment of youthful voyeurism: perched on top of a toilet in the back of the restaurant, gazing through a secret peephole, his eyes darting furtively. The young Deborah (Jennifer Connelly) is dancing, practising her ballet. Leone lets us know that she knows she is being watched; it becomes obvious that, instantly, her narcissistic joy in her own performance is doubled by this manipulative act of exhibitionism. Eventually, with her back to him, she starts to undress.

The film returns to the same space and the same dramatic set-up – Noodles on the toilet, the gramophone playing, Deborah about to rehearse alone – five scenes later. Except that this time she interrupts his secretive, voyeuristic reverie with a cruel, knowing taunt. Then Deborah leads Noodles on a kind of courtly dance through the various rooms and

Deborah is watched, and watches herself

An unbridgeable abyss: Deborah reads the 'Song of Songs' to Noodles

passageways of this empty place – the same place, we remember, to which the old Noodles has returned in 1968. Deborah is in complete control of this dance; Noodles scurries behind her like a frightened, silent pet. Finally, she invites him to sit beside her as she reads a passage from the 'Song of Songs', an illustration that sacred prayer can take place even in the most earthly settings. Again she toys with him, alternating phrases of fond, erotic praise ('his body is as bright ivory') with acerbic reminders of his filthy hygiene. She concludes her oration with one of the most biting lines of the film: 'He's altogether lovable, but he'll always be a two-bit punk, so he'll never be my beloved. What a shame.'

Leone uses one of the most basic figures of classical film grammar – the shot-reverse shot cross-cutting between faces – to expressive effect in this 'Song of Songs' exchange. The images take us closer than we have previously been to these two young, would-be lovers; but we are simultaneously frustrated because the shots keep them rigidly apart from one another, denying us a moment of real union. Finally – after an agonising volley of cuts between them being silent – Noodles moves in for a kiss. But it is instantly interrupted: now it's Max at the toilet slit, and he is there to call Noodles away for some rough, street business. Deborah once more adopts a steely posture, and the scene ends with a lingering, intimate shot of her angry face.

Later, only violence will be able to cross the yawning, taunting distance between these two characters – the most terrible, sexualised violence of rape which Noodles foists upon Deborah in the back of the chauffeured Rolls Royce. This is the awful, crowning moment of what Kaminsky refers to as their 'violent night' together.[47] If there is a masochistic drive in Noodles' distant, yearning, voyeuristic gazes – and in his shamed acknowledgment that he is indeed a two-bit punk forever below his revered love-object – then that masochism is finally, irrevocably, exchanged for sadism in the act of rape. And the strictly coarse, pulp logic of male fantasy that one might sense coursing through the film has a proudly sadistic rationale to offer for this rape: it's been coming for a long time, since childhood, when Noodles exclaimed to his buddies that if Deborah, with her wiles and put-downs, 'don't leave me alone, I'm gonna give her what she's asking for'.

But there is too much sadness, too much pain in this film for that to be the final, critical word on the violent culmination of this tawdry romance. The protracted rape scene in *Once Upon a Time in America* is not easy to watch, nor to discuss. It is really not one of those perversely thrilling rapes – where the woman supposedly comes to enjoy herself – in the vein of Peckinpah's *Straw Dogs* (1971). It is not spectacular in any galvanising, triumphant, sadistic or vulgar sense. Leone's gruesome set-piece has the cold, chilling tone of the pack-rape in *I Spit on Your Grave* (1980), or a teenage boy's violation of his drugged-out acquaintance in Larry Clark's *Kids* (1995), or Harvey Keitel's clumsy penetration of a gangster's moll in the women's toilet in James Toback's *Fingers* (1977) – all scenes, pointedly, deprived of musical accompaniment.

But why show this act at all? Is this scene (as some have complained) Leone's apologia for rape – some simple assertion that the boy can't help it? I do not believe so. *Once Upon a Time in America* offers, in many respects, a desolate and anguished portrait of male sexuality. Masculinity, as learnt and lived, is presented as an impossible, self-cancelling human condition. I do not believe that Leone deploys the women in the film as scapegoats for this desolation – even if Noodles, locked within the vicious circle of his own male complexes, does. From the earliest pubescent scenes, Noodles' sexuality is marked by wretchedness, impotence, repression, and a tearing gap between oceanic desire and its physical fulfilment. The harshest statement of this comes in the rooftop scene where Noodles and Max interrupt the tryst of the cop Whitey (Richard Foronji) with Peggy (Julie Cohen) and frame him with the evidence: after his experience of premature ejaculation with Peggy, Noodles gazes sadly as Max, the superior 'performer', enjoys himself at a more leisurely pace. And let us not overlook the grim irony of Leone staging Noodles' single uncomplicated fuck in the back of a hearse with a whore initially disguised as a naked corpse!

The scenes leading up to Noodles' rape of Deborah are among the film's most emotionally charged. They carry on what Lesley Stern calls the '*frissons* of romance'[48] – of perpetually deferred, unfulfilled consummation – established in the 'Song of Songs' scene. Again, there is that troubling interplay between the hushed intimacy of this couple and the increasingly large gulf between them. The growing class difference between Deborah and Noodles is insisted upon with some cruelty by Leone; we witness Noodles anxiously negotiating table manners while watched by a toffy restaurant waiter. As an on-site orchestra plays 'Amapola' under the scene, Deborah speaks of her aspirations: 'I've got

The violent night

to get to where I'm going … to the top.' Each time she attempts to discuss her ambitions, he flinches, withdraws, becomes defensive or aggressive – and she, in response, softens just a little, drops the subject.

The following scene, with them lying on the beach, twists the knife of these complex tensions still further. Noodles talks of his time in prison, how he endlessly recalled her Bible reading: 'Nobody's gonna love you the way I loved you.' And just as he is straining toward his impossible dream of a lifelong union between them she drops her bombshell: the announcement that, the following morning, she is leaving for Hollywood. So this is the emotional context in which the rape then occurs – this tragic collision of a woman who needs to follow her dream away from the potential partner for whom she has long-held, intense feelings, and a man whose capacity to express love and navigate its vicissitudes is blocked and deformed by all manner of deathly masculine neuroses.

It cannot be said strongly enough that Deborah is not a simple, two-dimensional stereotype in this depicted relationship – not merely some cipher of projective male fantasy. She does not have anything like the screen time that Noodles has, but she is none the less a vivid, full-blooded character. Part of this depth comes from the superb performance by Elizabeth McGovern. Leone clearly invests emotion and dignity in Deborah's yearning and her crisis, just as he does in Noodles' frustrated longings. The images are there to behold, and absorb: young Deborah, racked by a complex ambivalence, standing just inside the bar as Noodles rattles the door in anguish (a scene likely inspired by the ending of William Wyler's *The Heiress*, 1949); and adult Deborah, imbued with quiet loathing, staring coldly at the pathetic Noodles as she lowers the shade of the train carriage and cuts him out of her life for good.

Deborah's disappearance

7 'Been Goin' to Bed Early'

'Have you ever considered building your own haven, Mr Williams?'

Cemetery director (Louise Fletcher) to Noodles in scene cut from *Once Upon a Time in America*[49]

Going to the toilet is a sad business in *Once Upon a Time in America*. Early on during the 20s section, Noodles trundles up the stairs of the dishevelled apartment building where he lives with his folks. He indicates to Patsy (Brian Bloom) that he's about to head straight off to the toilet rather than step inside his home. Off-screen, we hear the sound of his parents bickering. Noodles glosses the situation for us: 'My old man's prayin' and my old lady's cryin'. And the light's turned off. What the hell should I go home for?' That is the only impression we ever receive of Noodles' home life and upbringing. The effect is brusque and disquieting, serving in a single stroke to indicate the extent of the hero's displacement from any conventional 'symbolic order' or human community.

'At least in here I can read': once inside the toilet, Noodles fetches a book he has hanging by a string outside the window (a curious ritual of secrecy) and settles down to read it, pants down around his ankles. It is *Martin Eden* by Jack London, a *Bildungsroman* popular with young male readers of another era. But it is the frontispiece of the book that matters, and a shot lingers on it in close-up: a portrait of a man and woman, who appear to be in riding clothes, sitting side by side in a rural setting. As so often, Leone gives us a wrenching contrast between romantic dreams and a miserable, all too real environment.

Earlier in the film we have already had another, even more poignant toilet scene. Moe exits, closes a door, and the wistful 'Deborah's Theme' begins; old Noodles begins to wander alone through this place of memories, as does Jean Simmons in the penultimate scene of Otto Preminger's *Angel Face* (1952). He looks again, longer and more intensely now, at the photo of the adult Deborah, and Leone's camera pans from the photo to him, grave and sorrowful, his face half cloaked in

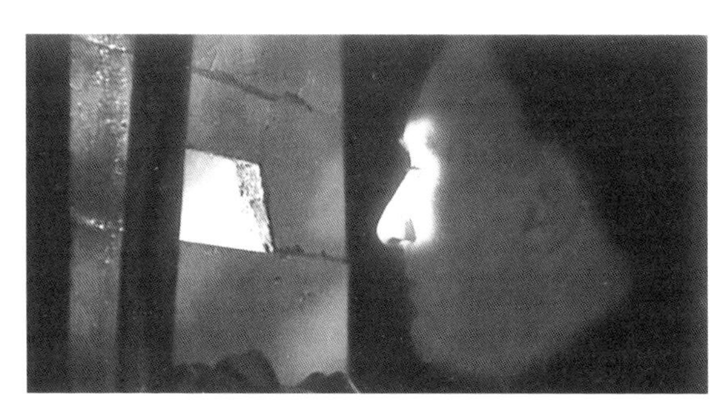

The old man as voyeur: Noodles at toilet slit

darkness. He flicks his eyes around the space as if to remind himself of where things are, orienting himself (a gesture superbly conveyed by De Niro), and then begins to move purposefully towards a door. In the background, the clock that has recently been restarted ticks solemnly.

What a screen moment this is: with the air full of unspoken matters and feelings so serious, with the singing voice of Edda Dell'Orso soaring on the soundtrack, Noodles steps into … a toilet. Nowhere in the film is the tension between sacred and profane, between sublime and earthy, between elevated, voluptuous desires and dirty, mundane, even shameful realities so exquisitely and tearingly caught. Noodles puts down the toilet seat and then, unexpectedly, stands on it. Facing the wall he opens a slit and, very slowly, leans into it. There is a sad, beautiful shot of Noodles' eyes seen through the slit, peering in, lit up – 'the old man as voyeur', as Kaminsky describes it.[50] The camera moves forward, eliminating the slits and framing only these eyes, as the jauntier 'Amapola' theme begins, and the long flashback to the 20s is triggered.

Flashback: young Noodles at the same slit

Once Upon a Time in America is surely among the most melancholic of films. This melancholy expresses itself not only through explicit narrative acts of betrayal and loss; it insinuates itself into every pore of the movie's texture, rhythm and mood. The epic feel of Leone's grand style had never before been so geared to the funereal. There is a weighty slowness to virtually every movement in the film, whether of people or objects: from the large, creaking, empty lift at Moe's that slowly rises to greet the waiting hood in an early scene, to the train that takes Deborah away from Noodles' defeated gaze; from the ominously yawning doors of the memorial crypt which Noodles visits to the heavy crawl of the black garbage truck in the penultimate scene.

Leone's cinematic rendering of time – and particularly his use of ellipses – plays an especially central role in creating this mood. Noodles' inaugural moment of decline – his introduction to a lifetime of sorrow – occurs when he is taken away to prison after the enraged stabbing of Bugsy. In a striking series of intercut, frontal, wordless tableaux, Noodles disappears from view, behind the vast gates of the jail. And he disappears from time too, 'gone in the splice' at the end of the shot, as Jacques Rivette once said of Carl Dreyer's *Gertrud* (1964).[51] In *Once Upon a Time in America* time not seen passing on screen,

The mission: Noodles finds a key in the mausoleum

time elided, is effectively the sign of a life not lived, a life absented or stolen.

There is so much dead time eating away at the figure of Noodles. He loses a month in the opium den after raping Deborah, and limps back to Max and the gang to face recriminations and ultimatums. He loses six years, his young adulthood, in that jail after the stabbing. And then he loses thirty-five years after the apparent death of Max, thirty-five years of obscurity without glory, love, pleasure or wealth. Such hollowed-out time brings with it what Jonathan Rosenbaum dubs 'haunted memory' – and a particular, often harsh pathos found in films ranging from *The Magnificent Ambersons* (1942) to *India Song* (1974).[52]

A stolen life: young Noodles off to jail

The melancholy of Leone's film is also inextricably bound up with its presentation of masculinity. Noodles' vision, his male gaze – contrary to a certain assumption of 70s feminist film theory – orders nothing, effects nothing. When he looks longingly across a distance, his gaze marks only that distance, and the unbridgeable emotional abyss which it represents. And, more profoundly, he is one of the archetypal male sleepwalkers of modern cinema, a ghost or zombie on a par with Willem Dafoe in *Light Sleeper* (Paul Schrader, 1991) or Jack Nicholson in *The Crossing Guard* (Sean Penn, 1995). This is the meaning and resonance of the line when, on his fateful return to the bar, Noodles replies to Moe's question about what he has been doing since 1933 with five little words that speak volumes: 'Been goin' to bed early.'

The shadow or reminder of death is everywhere in this film – and its traces are not confined to scenes of Noodles as an old man. Rolando Caputo has pointed out that 'a set of metaphors and motifs about sleep and death … traverse the character's destiny.'[53] This set includes: the bullet-holed outline that Eve finds in the first scene; the sex scene in the back of a hearse; the torn-up grave stones; and the tomb which Noodles visits that contains a plaque in his name. Part of the dark poetry of this lost hero's reappearance at Moe's bar derives from the fact that the establishment has previously been identified as 'the joint that never closes' – and here is Noodles, like some angel of death, instantly bringing down its shutters and closing its doors. Or perhaps more exactly, Noodles is a figure who has been called back to life from the realm of the dead, woken up from his big sleep.

Once Upon a Time in America is a tale of male pathos. First, there is the fact that Noodles is – as he himself declares – a 'loser' from one end of the story to the other. At every point of his path, he is suckered and snookered. No one in the gang suffers quite like Noodles: it is he who gets sent to jail as an adolescent, he who suffers all the difficult pangs of love in his pining for Deborah. Noodles' story thus embodies one of the principal forms of masculine pathos in contemporary western culture: he is an eternal victim whose very life is stolen from him, and (to make matters even worse) stolen by a duplicitous male rival who betrays his love.

To the familiar pathos of the stolen life is added the sad moonglow of a half life. There is a cinema of twilight, a cinema of half lives, half lived. This cinema traditionally belongs to the person wide-eyed at the window, key-hole or movie screen – the stranger in paradise. Outwardly passive, the stranger in fact watches and listens and thinks furiously; and, above all, he yearns. There is no beyond to which death might release him; the vision of earthly, earthy life, just over there, forever out of reach, is all the heaven he desires. Noodles is one such stranger in paradise, in the company of Wim Wenders' circling, listening angels in *Wings of Desire* (1987). And it is no accident, I suspect, if any or all of these loners, in their ghostly half lives, remind us of a typical cinephile, immersed in the imaginary worlds of movies.

But there is a tougher, more agonised side to the pathos in *Once Upon a Time in America*, as there is in Scorsese's *Raging Bull* (1980) and Abel Ferrara's *Bad Lieutenant* (1992). Noodles is a particular kind of male archetype: the dumb animal. The dumbness is not so much a lack of brains as a lack of self-consciousness – a fatal inability to see, judge and change himself. Noodles grasps only one thing about himself: that he is a loser, a no-hoper, a poor bastard (the maudlin refrain of many a tale of male pathos) – a maligned victim of some cosmic system of destiny that is utterly beyond his ken. Thus, he is the classic 'blind man' of film melodrama, the man who colludes in his own misery and oppression by mistaking the socially constructed ideology of his beleaguered masculinity as his biological destiny.

Yet it is doubtful whether Leone would retain any vestige of radical, reformist hope for his anti-hero. Because Noodles is also an animal: an unsocialised, unsocialisable bundle of drives and desires. A propensity for violence and loss of control is, in Leone's men, a kind of original sin: they are born with it, and must suffer with the consequences of that primal, inner scar. Acts of uncontrolled, uncontrollable excess form a motif in the film, from Patsy's gorging himself on cake and the young Noodles' impulsive knifing of a cop, to Max's psychotic reaction to being called crazy and the rape that alienates Noodles from Deborah for a lifetime. In this light, Dominic's dying words about 'slipping' take

on a particular resonance, and an uncannily prophetic power. Male energy, in Leone's portrayal, is forever out of gear, thrusting blindly, unreconcilable, animalistic. Yet it is not simply or unproblematically a vicious energy, pure aggro. What makes Noodles precisely a pathetic character is that his violence is entwined, in ways he can never understand or control, with his intense, oceanic feelings of love, lust and loyalty.

Central to the film's portrait of masculinity is a feeling of torment, something ambivalent, tearing, wretched. It is a strange and plaintive moment in cinema history, this surge of male melancholia that reaches a peak with Leone's last film. It is as if the cinema, so often pegged as a patriarchal apparatus designed to flatter, glorify and arouse the male viewer, found one of its rendezvous with destiny by in fact describing (with indelible, heart-rending accuracy) the breakdown of that very apparatus, through tales of men variously repressed, impotent, mournful or tragically, ineffectually violent.

Catching up: Moe and Noodles see Jimmy on TV

8 For a Few Minutes More (Or Less)

All the great manipulators of the audience – from Hitchcock to Tati, from Chaplin to Leone – have also been great logicians, who gambled on the pride which we had every right to feel – as viewers – when we had learned to see, to deduce, to imagine, on the basis of the rebus they offered us.

Serge Daney, 1992[54]

Leone suspected, as he was editing his epic, that he was going to run into problems with its American release. The distribution contract with the Ladd Company for America and Canada specified a length of 165 minutes. The idea of releasing the film in two separate parts was originally considered but quickly abandoned. As Leone's fine cuts crawled up to 228 minutes, Ladd Company executives started sensing 'exhibitor resistance' to a product of such length. A test preview of Leone's version in Boston in February 1984 proved a disaster from the Ladd Company's point of view, and so it set about progressively shortening, altering and re-testing the film with audiences. So, the infamous 147 minute 'American cut' – with all the scenes rearranged into a linear chronology so as to avoid the 'confusions' engendered in the initial test audience by Leone's narrative structure – opened in the United States in June 1984, scarcely days after the European premiere at Cannes of Leone's version. The director did not take these developments well; he immediately initiated a protracted legal battle with Milchan and the Ladd Company.

As Adam Knee has documented in his illuminating study of the American reception of the short version, a number of respected critics were moved to some odd pronouncements about the strengths and deficiencies of Leone's art. Andrew Sarris, sceptical that the original version was necessarily any better than the altered one, reflected that 'Leone has never been a master of narrative'. Mal Vincent went further: 'Logical plotting is not his forte even under the best of conditions. … One suspects that Warner Bros. has done the film good instead of harm.'[55] And, in what is perhaps the most perverse moment in the annals of film criticism, Mary Corliss argued that, 'under Ladd's instructions, an editor named Zach Staenburg reshaped Leone's mesmerizing, intermittently powerful botch of a movie into a … film that is within shooting distance of masterpiece.'[56] Her conclusions – that the shorter film 'makes more sense', has 'considerably more emotive force' and is a 'stronger, more cohesive film'[57] – are not judgments that I believe can be reasonably sustained. To this lover of *Once Upon a Time in America*, the short version is an utterly abject viewing experience.

Eighty-one minutes were cut from the film. Included in this block are many entire scenes, and one major plot thread. When Deborah leaves by train in the 30s, she never returns – thus eliminating everything to do with the tortured 'family romance' configuring Noodles, Max, Deborah and David. The scenes introducing young Max and establishing the dynamic of his relationship with Noodles are gone. Also cut from the 20s section is the scene of the gang in a restaurant looking to 'roll a drunk', and the thematically crucial rooftop scene involving Noodles, Max, the cop and Peggy. From the 1968 section, scenes of Noodles arriving at the train station, walking the streets, experiencing paranoia at night as he carries the suitcase of money, and conversing with Carol in the rest home, have all been excised. A great many more parts of the film were ruthlessly trimmed: Noodles and Deborah at the restaurant; Noodles' return to Moe's; the party at the Bailey mansion. The chronological reshuffling has a devastating effect on the rhythm of scenes – some highlights (such as Deborah's youthful dance or Patsy's devouring of cake) now seem interminable and ungainly. In fact, the whole film, in this version, alternates between *longueurs* and piecemeal scene fragments.

In the first place, this trimming appears to have been in the service of a certain 'toning down' of the material – all scenes of violence (including sexual violence) have been considerably lessened in their impact. But also, the trimming follows that misguided logic which deems that only plot (or 'narrative drive') matters – thus rendering the film as a skeleton that lacks all its funereal rhythms, and many of its dramatic nuances (as, for instance, in the cemetery sequence, where the entire poetic construction of spatial relations and sound atmospheres has been grossly simplified). In the short version, virtually all the poetic high-points of the film are gone. What are properly the first scenes – that delicate initiation into the dream and map of the film – now appear over an hour in, their aesthetic function completely robbed. The sound of the ringing phone has been removed, and the shots comprising that magisterial montage re-distributed. Noodles' old eyes at the toilet slit are gone, as is the finale in the opium den. Parts of scenes that are primarily reflective or symbolic in function – such as Noodles' lone venturing into the feather cleaning plant – are discarded.

Many stylistic elements, and even specific plot details, were drastically rejigged. Music cues are routinely shifted for every re-cut scene, and the music itself is often brutally shortened. Extra, 'explanatory' lines of dialogue are added in pauses where the original is wordless. Many sound effects – particularly such expressionistic Leone touches as a piercing train whistle when the adult Noodles opens the empty suitcase at the station – have been replaced. Anything resembling an establishing shot (a wide shot of a street, for instance) is shuttled to the beginning of a scene. Shots from different scenes are occasionally combined in the one scene. Even the final scene at the Bailey mansion is altered: in place of the pulp poetry of a body in the blades of a garbage truck (to Corliss, a 'very questionable ending'),[58] the short version unfussily dubs an off-screen gun-shot sound over an available close-up of Noodles standing outside the mansion.[59]

Where the shorter version of *Once Upon a Time in America* is a horrendous reality still circulating on American cable television, the existence of a longer version is a myth. From the moment of the film's Cannes premiere, Leone was happy to boast about an extra forty-five minutes of splendid material that he had reluctantly decided to cut in order to arrive at his 228 minutes – tantalisingly stating in the next breath that this material would be reinstated for an Italian TV mini-series version circa 1987.

But no official longer version of the film was ever actually constituted and completed, either by Leone or any his collaborators after his death in 1989. Certainly – as is routinely the case with most films –

A bad end: the mulching gears of the garbage truck

more scenes were scripted and shot than were included in the final cut. Some scenes may have been only partially edited by Nino Baragli; some may have travelled as far as the next-to-final cut but never received proper post-production work. If we momentarily ignore such cold film-making realities, however, an aggregate image can be collated from material included in a 322 page draft of the screenplay,[60] and from various production accounts, of the mythical long version of *Once Upon a Time in America*.

Material not included in the finished product runs the gamut of all the different kinds of scenes contained in the film: gangsterish exploits (including a dialogue-less scene in which Max and Noodles, disguised as workmen, case the Federal Bank); scenes of character interaction both melancholic and dramatic; scenes that reiterate or extend the central poetic metaphors of the film; and expressionistic conceits devised for the time transitions. An example of the last category is a scene expanding Noodles' hasty exit from New York at the end of the film's opening movement. Noodles hitches a ride with a truck driver and arrives at a level crossing; a long train that is transporting cars approaches, filling the entire frame. The cars on the train are, at first, 1933 Fords; by the time we see the end of the train, they are of a 60s make. When the train clears the frame, we see Noodles, thirty-five years older, returning to New York City on the same road. It was at this point that the title was to have appeared on screen, instead of at the very start.

In the 20s section, the scene in which Noodles arrives home and reads in the toilet was preceded by a scene with his family – a father, mother and kid brother all absent from the finished film. Noodles enters enraged, shouting at his mother for food. The scene reads as a slightly cartoonish take on 'Goldilocks and the Three Bears': finding only a cockroach-covered, empty bowl on the dining table, Noodles hurls himself accusingly upon his brother, and then realises that his father is the one who has stolen his meal. Noodles' father has evidently withdrawn from the material world of work and money; he fasts and prays obsessively. As the light in the apartment flickers out (there is no quarter for the meter), Noodles exits to the toilet with his copy of *Martin Eden*, arguing with his downtrodden mother: 'I ain't gonna end up like him.' What Kaminsky recalls as 'probably the funniest scene in the film' involved the gang in the 30s on an airplane to Detroit from New York for their jewellery store robbery. The gang members have smuggled gin onto the plane and proceed to have a party; the other passengers at first show their disapproval but conclude by joining in the merriment. On the page, the scene has a rousing, populist, Capraesque flavour.

Leone was candid about the fact that progressive work on the film tended to reduce 'much that concerned relationships with women'.[61] The script expands, for instance, the violent night between Noodles and Deborah. Before meeting up, Noodles watches Deborah on stage in a musical revue, 'singing and dancing and dazzling with class and beauty' – another in the long and complex series of gazes across the film. Then, just prior to Deborah's arrival at the car, Noodles has an exchange with the chauffeur, a Jewish refugee from Germany. This scene – which Kaminsky regarded as crucial – was shot with producer Arnon Milchan in the role; Leone described it as 'very beautiful' and lamented its loss from the final cut.[62] In it, the chauffeur indicates to Noodles the contempt with which his gang is regarded by the general Jewish community:

CHAUFFEUR: Noodles – of Max, Noodles and Company. Everybody knows you.
NOODLES: You don't approve?
CHAUFFEUR: It's your business.
NOODLES: Come on, let's hear it.

CHAUFFEUR: I can't say. You take the Italians. They look up to their Mafia, their godfathers. With Jews it's different.
NOODLES: Max, Noodles and Company are the black sheep of the ghetto.[63]

In relation to its female characters, the film as it stands displays a particularly stunning lacuna: the introduction of Eve, who simply appears without explanation beside Noodles at the Florida beach. In the script, she is introduced between Noodles' rape of Deborah, and the scene of the latter's departure by train the following morning. Distraught, Noodles sits at a bar getting blind drunk and Eve, a prostitute, approaches him. He pays her a thousand dollars on the condition that he can 'call her Deborah' during love-making. Back in his hotel room, however, he quickly passes out after reciting a few lines from the previously quoted 'Song of Songs'. In the morning he awakes alone and finds a note from Eve ('so long – and thanks. Deborah'). This scene contains several of the film's key motifs and themes, such as Noodles' 'dead sleep' and his wilful, desperate forgetfulness. Then follows a prologue to the train station scene: Noodles arrives and, once again, gazes impotently at Deborah as she finishes breakfast and moves to the train. This part of the sequence, highly regarded by Leone, was filmed at the Brasserie Julien in Paris.

Eve next appears in the script after the hospital room scene with Jimmy and the other gang members. Noodles bumps into her in the lift going downstairs; she refreshes his dim memory of their night together. He takes her once again to his hotel room; the prelude to their sex involves a playful bit of banter, derived from Grey's novel, that reveals Eve's 'falsies' – one of several references to visual illusions (and their unmasking) throughout the film. The following morning, another round of banter and sex is suddenly and threateningly interrupted by Max bursting into the room and exclaiming 'Let's go to the beach' – a scene documented in an oft-reproduced production still. Finally, in the scene in which Noodles betrays Max over the phone at the speakeasy, there is an extended farewell dialogue between Eve and Noodles.[64]

In the 1968 section of the script, Noodles' search for the truth about his mysterious situation is more gradual. An early scene in the

A cut scene: Max surprises Noodles and Eve in bed

office of a synagogue, a dialogue between Noodles and a secretary, establishes the location of the gang members' graves. After Noodles finds the key at the mausoleum, he is approached by the cemetery director; this scene was shot with Louise Fletcher in the role. Beyond its strict plot function – to deepen the mystery and intrigue – this extended dialogue has the woman (referring to Noodles by his alias 'Mr Williams' throughout) speak of tombs as 'havens' and explain the Egyptian 'cult of death'. These references resonate with many elements, including Noodles' opium taking and Deborah's on-stage role as Cleopatra.

Jimmy's role in the 30s and 60s sections was reduced between script and final cut. Material detailing his calling of a factory strike, and the beginnings of his collusion with organised crime, was condensed. In the script, an exchange between Jimmy and Max in the latter's study precedes the dialogue between Noodles and Max. The ironies of political history are spelt out by Jimmy: 'I've avoided making mistakes and you haven't. You're stupid, and, unfortunately, you're also in the way.' This leads to Jimmy's unsubtle suggestion to Max that he kill himself – 'I'd be very happy for you if tonight, during all the noise of the party, I heard a shot' – to which Max replies: 'Maybe you will.'

One particular intervention, occurring during the subsequent, fateful exchange between Noodles and Max, appears in the final draft script, the novelisation, and the version shown in 1996 on British television, but not in any other cut of the film that I have seen. When Max takes out his gun from a desk drawer and slides it across to Noodles, the latter gazes at it and experiences a 'montage of memories'. In the script these are: young Max on the overloaded wagon, Max and Noodles at an amusement park, Max diving into the balloons popping up in the water, and then, in harsh contrast, the supposed corpse of Max, horribly disfigured. In the movie, the shots are all from the 20s: Max on wagon, Noodles calling for Max in the water, the gang members' hands on the suitcase, and the well-known poster image of the characters in front of the Brooklyn Bridge.

I much prefer the long version of the film that omits this montage. Beyond the fact that the delicately suspenseful atmosphere, sustained by an 'incidental' track of popular songs, is crudely broken by the insert, there is no other temporal jump in the film which is as utterly conventional as this one – i.e., an unambiguous flashback happening inside the protagonist's mind, staged via what Ronnie Scheib witheringly describes as the already old-fashioned 'zoom or dolly into an object quivering with its montage potential to leap to an ego-defining past'.[65] The cinematic poetry of *Once Upon a Time in America* depends upon a delicate ambiguity: every time the film dances elsewhere in time, we cannot say with certainty whether it is a character (Noodles) remembering, or the film itself taking its narrational liberty, cutting on the flicker of an association or a motif. We cannot exactly say whether this dizzy and hallucinatory film proceeds, is called up, from Noodles' vision, or the auteur Leone's vision – or maybe our own vision, seduced, made complicit, enchanted by such a cunning rebus. *Once Upon a Time in America* is a film, like all films, 'cut to the measure of desire', as Laura Mulvey once suggested[66] – but whose desire exactly, or better, what web of murky, shared, interwoven desires?

9 Pillar of Salt

Between the noticeable dramatic lines of De Niro's face, there is a shimmering of some love of what film can be.

Stan Brakhage, 1994[67]

A thin, echoing version of 'Deborah's Theme' begins as the old Noodles looks at a photo of Deborah that proudly adorns the home for the elderly where Carol now lives. The scene that follows is the reunion of Noodles and Deborah, thirty-five years after their violent night and parting morning. She has become a famous actress, and Noodles has just watched her triumphant performance in Shakespeare's *Antony and Cleopatra*. Noodles will also, in this scene, have his suspicion confirmed that Deborah is Bailey's lover. The central enigma that drives the scene – Noodles' angry question to Deborah, 'Who is Secretary Bailey?' – will finally be answered by a visual, physical revelation: David ('His name's David, just like yours,' speaks Deborah solemnly) is the spitting image of the young Max. This moment of revelation is, on many levels, the heart of Leone's film.

But before that coda there is the long dialogue between Deborah and Noodles in her dressing room. This scene begins, as the very start of

A game of masks: Deborah and Noodles in her dressing room

the film did, in darkness: it is the rich black of Deborah's backstage dressing gown, which is soon whisked away from the lens by her action of sitting down. Recalling *The Magnificent Ambersons*, Leone pushes his ode to haunted memory further towards the stylistic poles of stillness, darkness and silence as its apocalyptic conclusion draws nigh. It is not exactly the face we just saw in the photo that concluded the previous scene: Deborah is made up in extravagant, exaggerated white-face. Before this mirror, attempting to hold her composure during the exchange that follows, inner signs of anger and sorrow both hidden by and mingling with her disappearing layers of make-up, Deborah is truly an iconic movie apparition, an uncanny composite of all those sad male clowns fighting back their tears (such as Charlie Chaplin in *Limelight*, 1952) and Jean Seberg, melting with the pain of recall as she paints her face at the start and end of Preminger's *Bonjour Tristesse* (1957).

What is happening in this scene? Of all the dance-like interactions between these two characters choreographed by Leone, this one is the most funereal. The highly theatrical staging of the action uses in-frame lamps, a large mirror, and a cluttered space that seems to retard or impede free bodily movement: given Deborah's make-up, we are witnessing a literal instance of the Leonesque 'game of masks'. The scene kicks over the ashes of a romance that never was, a love that went horribly wrong and could never be saved or revived. Noodles clearly has more of a sense, now, of the monstrosity, the wrong-headed betrayal involved in his past behaviour towards her; he wonders aloud whether her first words will be 'I was hopin' never to see you again'. But nothing of love or rape, regret or loss, yearning or healing, is directly spoken of in this exchange. Their dialogue begins formally, with questions that yield only brusque, cryptic or evasive answers. (Him: You live alone? Her: No. … You staying? Him: That depends.)

After these terse volleys, the words soften for a moment. Noodles praises Deborah's performance on stage, and blesses her life-choice. But when he starts quizzing her about the party to which he has been invited on Long Island, the sweet music ends and the mood turns ugly. He presses on with his interrogation; she gets flustered. She goes

into a trance as she recites the 'official' biography of Bailey; finally he snaps and asks: 'Why can't you tell me that you've been living with him all these years, and that you're his lover?' But still she will not say everything.

Deborah tries as hard as possible at first to hide the awful truth from Noodles, and then – when this proves impossible – to dissuade him from going any further in his quest for knowledge. This frankly grandiloquent scene now reaches its strangely ceremonial, ritual, mythic point. 'All we have left now are our memories,' she tells him. 'If you go to that party on Saturday night, you won't have those any more.' And – having heard David's voice from outside – she pleads with Noodles to leave via a side exit. He asks, 'Are you afraid that I'll turn into a pillar of salt?', and she replies: 'If you go out that door, yes.'

The following series of shots – perhaps the gravest of the film – forms a sequence that effortlessly bridges two different scenes in two locations. Noodles and David (introduced by a zoom in) stare at each other. After a long and painful moment of recognition on Noodles' part, he leaves; David gestures, with a puzzled expression, to Deborah, who appears utterly broken by this drama. Then there is a long moment of blackness upon the screen again, as Morricone's music ('Deborah's

A moment of revelation: David gazes at Noodles

Theme' again, cued by Noodles' line about the pillar of salt) soars, and finally a slow camera movement shows us old Max opening his upstairs window, looking down on and waving to his still carefree son. Some carping viewers ask: how could Noodles have come this far in modern day New York without cottoning on to the fact that Bailey is in fact his old comrade? But this is a fairy tale for adults, as Leone insisted, and the tale demands the suspension of disbelief that allows this magisterial moment of visual and dramatic revelation.

Among everything else that it achieves, this sequence is a testament to a great actor. Leone knew that working with De Niro was going to be a different and more collaborative actor–director relation than any he was used to: 'for better or worse, I had worked actors like marionettes. ... So for the first time, in this film, I have had to follow an actor's ideas without destroying my own. Yes, Bobby will have his *interpretazione artistica*.'[68]

Going for a swim: Max and Noodles argue

In the event, one of the most remarkable achievements of the art and craft of *Once Upon a Time in America* is the perfect meshing of Leone's style and De Niro's 'artistic interpretation'. All of Leone's films – no less than Dreyer's or Visconti's or Téchiné's – are odes to the human face. The face as ever-changing landscape, as *tabula rasa*, as comic punctuation, or as the still point that absorbs and reflects the deepest, unspoken truths of the drama at its highest moments: Leone's cinema is a veritable portrait gallery of such diversely expressive faces, from all the ornery cowboys who step into frame to blot out the natural landscape in the Westerns to the poignant freeze-frame on a childlike, wide-eyed, perplexed Rod Steiger at the end of *Giu la testa*.

De Niro, for his part, gives one of the finest performances of his career – but how atypical it is in many ways, so different from his

Eyes wide shut: Noodles gazes back at David

signature work with Scorsese. We tend to associate this actor with a certain restless, explosive energy: from De Palma's early films to *Cape Fear* (1991), he inhabits the frame like a restless, caged animal. What is different about De Niro in Leone's film is the extreme control and restraint imposed on his abundant physical power. Noodles, although a gangster, is the most inward, the least active character that De Niro has ever played. His energy is channelled into very specific, concentrated bodily zones: his head (shaken, lowered, raised) and especially his eyes. De Niro's eye movements have never been so intense or busy as in *Once Upon a Time in America*. At particular moments of emotional stress, when his head in close-up is absolutely still – such as when he looks at young David, a look that is held on screen for an agonisingly prolonged thirty seconds – his eyes dart about in such a way as to reveal an immense interior anguish.

Jean-Claude Carrière speaks of the element of mystery in filmic images where an actor gives a pointed, poignant gaze: 'A look … is very strong, precise, is meaningful, but in the same time, for certain spectators, it is ambiguous.'[69] In the dressing room scene and its immediate aftermath, every look – Noodles', Deborah's, David's, Max's – carries a charged and terrifying ambiguity.

10 | Say It Here and I Deny It Here

Every performance has three sides to it – mine, yours, and the truth.

Deborah to Noodles, dressing room scene, in draft script of *Once Upon a Time in America*[70]

Standing on the street outside the Bailey mansion after the Mac truck has passed, Noodles sees an apparition which is disjointed from the natural, linear flow of time: a cavalcade of partygoers, dressed in 30s garb, revelling while the same recording of 'God Bless America' heard during the opening credits plays again, booming from a car radio. The cavalcade passes Noodles by, and the noise of the music fades out at the end of the street. Then, from a close-up of his blank, inscrutable face, we are taken somewhere completely unexpected: back to the opium den, with its shadow puppets and oriental bric-a-brac. The young adult Noodles enters; from his clothes, we can gather that it is probably that same night which began the film, the night of his comrades' death. Or, more broadly, this retreat to drugged, somnambulant anonymity could well be Leone's metaphor for those thirty-five years of seclusion when Noodles 'went to bed early'.

Whenever or however we choose to think this scene is taking place, it is still an odd conclusion. The film has taken us suddenly from a moment of narrative closure to a moment of indeterminacy and openness; it has wrenched us from the historical stage of social, interpersonal relations and deposited us in a privatised, subjective space; and, above all, it has chosen a lyrical farewell that is marked by reverie, fantasy and hallucination.

Noodles moves through the den slowly, hangs up his coat, seats himself, and waits for the thin, little man who prepares his opium pipe. Lying down, Noodles starts puffing frantically, desperately: the contortion of the muscles in his face suggests that this effort causes him a certain amount of pain, as it did in the earlier opium scene. In a wrenching, uncomfortable juxtaposition, Morricone's title theme here builds to its paroxysmic height: the orchestra reaches a crescendo, and

that piercing voice of Edda Dell'Orso carries the melody line to some expressive, melodramatic register beyond mere language.

Noodles starts to turn so as to lay on his back, and then the film cuts to its final image. It is an overhead image, shot through a net – reminiscent of Josef von Sternberg's lovely, poignant images of Dietrich as Catherine the Great, always framed and encased by various nets and veils in *The Scarlet Empress* (1934), and also of a key, overhead shot of Claudia Cardinale filmed through a net in *Once Upon a Time in the West*. For the last time in this film and in his career, Leone utilises his beloved zoom lens to slowly take us into the universe that is De Niro's face. First, the face is perfectly impassive; then it completely re-shapes itself into an enormous, even grotesque smile, a great clown face of bliss and abandon. On the bursting forth of that smile, Morricone's music swells again, and quickly modulates into a long, wistful resolution of 'Deborah's Theme'. The frozen image of that face remains, like the music, until the very end of the closing credits. Noodles is now suspended in some place, some 'atopia' beyond time, beyond narrative.

Leone was well aware that this ending opens up the possibility of what he called a 'double reading' of the film.[71] Looping back to the night at the opium den in this way can suggest that everything in the strict

Noodles sucks desperately on the opium pipe

chronology of the plot – specifically, all the events of the 60s – is a fabrication by Noodles, who has 'imagined the entire core of the film as a fantasy to relieve himself of the responsibility for the death of his friends'.[72] This was an interpretation that apparently pleased Leone immensely. He even suggested that the time-jumping structure of the film could itself be understood as the agitated, backwards and forwards motion of Noodles' mind in the throes of its 'opium dream'. But it is important to note that, whenever he raised these matters, Leone would add a phrase that he was fond of using in relation to many topics, a phrase that translates roughly as: 'I say it here, and I deny it here.' For him the double reading, this oscillation between literal and subjective levels of representation, had to remain open.

The question that has dogged the reception of art cinema classics from *Otto e mezzo* (1963) and *Belle de Jour* (1967) to *Barton Fink* (1991) and *Naked Lunch* (1991) – 'Is what we see real, or just a dream?' – is in many respects a banal non-question. Solving the matter one way or another is ultimately not very interesting or illuminating. But nor is it enough to simply assert that all films are ultimately dream-like, that cinema is of its essence oneiric. The double reading that articulates the realms of dream and reality can have a mystery, a tension – in short, a

Idiot grin: Noodles escapes into his dream

content. Leone's film belongs to that dynamic textual space which Raymond Bellour sees inaugurated in Ritwik Ghatak's masterpiece *Meghe Dhaka Tara* (*The Cloud-Capped Star*, 1960): 'The cinema is recognised here in its ever-tested limit, so difficult to touch, between interior and exterior, realist image and mental image, perception and hallucination.'[73]

But let's follow, for a moment, Leone's speculation that the film is a purely subjective 'dream-journey', and that this dream functions psychologically and emotionally for Noodles as 'a haven and a refuge'[74] – in other words as a phantasm, an imaginary resolution of real problems, a way to heal his sore wounds. Kaminsky puts it eloquently: 'Is the whole tale, bookended by the opium scene, an opium dream by Noodles, a dream in which what he projects as a wasted life will be justified in the future, in which, in fantasy, he will discover that he did not betray his friends at all but was, himself, the tragic victim who becomes the tragic hero?'[75]

Particularly in these days when the 'mythic journeys' of hero-figures are strenuously advocated in screenwriting manuals, it is tempting to put an upbeat, almost New Age gloss on *Once Upon a Time in America*. Kaminsky leans towards such a view. For him, the film 'suggests that the power of the fairy tale, the myth, the fantasy is to bring the viewer and Noodles to an ultimate reality'.[76] Noodles ends the film in a haze, bereft of any connections to other people, but he has attained a certain inner peace, a putting to rest of his own demons. His final smile is, in this sense, genuine, full, transparent. (The novelisation of the film by Lee Hays contrives an even more up-beat conclusion: his version of the tale dispenses with the opium den coda altogether, and ends with Noodles outside the Bailey mansion, simply 'walk[ing] away from it all'!)[77]

Among commentators, Michel Chion has taken the most strictly psychoanalytic angle on this dream-journey which the film offers us. He is drawn – it is hard not to be – by the one strikingly unrealistic detail in the 60s section of the film: the apparent eternal youthfulness of Deborah, as revealed once the make-up has come off, in the dressing room scene. There is more going on here than a simple sentimentalising or idealising of female beauty.

For Chion, this is the central scene of the film. He associates Leone's cinematic time machine with the literal tales of time travel found in science fiction and fantasy cinema. He reminds us that time travel stories (such as *Back to the Future*, 1985) often play out 'Oedipal phantasms of a man's encounter with his mother' before the proper father enters the scene. And so, in this key scene of *Once Upon a Time in America*, we have the crystallisation of a luridly melodramatic fantasy-scenario, lurking underneath the strict, literal logic of the plot, that harks back to the terrible rape scene, as if to rewrite its outcome: Deborah as beautiful as she was at that moment, the 'mother beyond time', and 'Max-2, the clone' as the fruit of their union.[78] For Chion, Noodles is thus 'the person without real roots who pursues in the beyond-space and beyond-time of an opium dream the phantasm of endlessly engendering himself'.[79] Naturally, the fact that he engenders himself as Max brings another perverse twist into this family romance: the child is the token of his homo-erotic love for Max, a desire that can only be worked out in a circuit that passes through the one woman they have both 'had'.

For me, Leone's film arrives at an emotional complexity which is intensely ambivalent and mysterious, far too much so for either the up-beat, transcendent reading or the gothic psycho-sexual interpretation to hold absolutely. I say it here and I deny it here: this might be the stance of *Once Upon a Time in America* towards all the thematic templates that it advances or suggests. In fact Chion suggests as much when he reminds us that the narrative construction of several of Leone's narratives rests upon what he calls an *anamnesis*, a recalling of things past.[80] This is a structure of subjectivity in which a primal trauma is both relived obsessively, and also erased, censored, cast into oblivion. There is a deathly quality to this complex, a stasis or desperate freezing which we can also recognise in Leone's finale – the director himself described the film as a 'dance of death in which a man moves towards forgetting'.[81] And there is a feeling of tension, even anguish – a sense of some horrible, crushing reality (like the face of 'Max-2') that must be feverishly barred or repressed by Noodles' psyche. What Tony Rayns calls Noodles' 'intact, and perfect' fantasy[82] depends on a massive blocking-out of what he has come to learn in the course of the film.

An opium habit is certainly a good device for expressing the ambivalent sum of these knotty psychic swirls. Drug taking is not a primary subject of *Once Upon a Time in America*, but the film joins a sombre group from *The Private Life of Sherlock Holmes* (Billy Wilder, 1970) to *J'entends plus la guitare* (Philippe Garrel, 1991) in which the central character's immersion in a drug experience spreads a pall over the entire text. A flight into the half life of intoxication is rendered as a withdrawal from the world. But this withdrawal involves a keen and painful paradox, for drugs simultaneously dull certain senses (particularly the sense of pain brought on by guilt or remorse) while heightening the 'sweet sadness' of one's general perceptions. This half life induced by drugs is a peculiarly cinematic state, a superbly artistic reverie. It helps Noodles to remake the world, at least in his mind.

Whatever gets Noodles through his long, dark night of the soul, he is certainly able to face Max in the film's penultimate scene in an eerily composed manner. The *mise en scène* of this denouement is superbly grave. It is another dance of bodies as we have seen many times previously in the film. But now the bodies belong to two aged men, and their movements are gradual, tempered, tense. Something threatens to explode all throughout the scene – some passion, hatred or recrimination – but it never does. At no point does Noodles ever openly acknowledge what he clearly now knows – the true identity of Max. He chooses instead to refuse all offers from his soul-brother by performing a charade of blissful ignorance, maintaining the fiction stage-managed by Max, referring to him throughout as 'Mr Bailey' or 'Mr Secretary'. Only once does something resembling bitterness or insult form itself in his words, at his parting line as he exits through a secret, side door: 'I hope the investigation turns out to be nothing – it'd be a shame to see a lifetime of work go to waste.'

What is the emotional dynamic, the sub-text, underlying and animating this terse, eleven minute exchange? History has turned on Max the master manipulator, but here, in the lonely hour of the final

instance, he tries to stage one last, perfect scene. It is his attempt to salvage a clean, unambiguous, generic ending to the story of himself and Noodles, to secure for them both the roles of gangsters with glory – however tarnished that glory. It is, after all, a classic gangster scenario which Max offers Noodles: 'the money and the contract', and – above all – an opportunity for ultimate revenge, a culmination to the cycle of masculine injuries and reprisals. Max is finally asking Noodles to take the place of a hero, to assume his role as an aggrieved, passionate man of action.

What Max offers Noodles here is a move, an act, without risk, repercussion or responsibility. So why doesn't he take it? What Noodles chooses to continue to live is his absolute loss of self, his passivity. He denies the possibility of action one more time, and withdraws. Isn't this the most melancholic ending of all? At the emotional highpoint of the scene, Noodles tells us the story of his life:

You see, Mr Secretary, I have a story also. It's a little simpler than yours. Many years ago I had a friend, a dear friend. I turned him in to save his life, but he was killed. But he wanted it that way. It was a great friendship. It went bad for him. It went bad for me, too.

Noodles exits by the secret door

Max still cannot take such implacability from Noodles, although he is now decades beyond the point where he once could knock him out in retaliation. But he at least asks, as he quietly boils over: 'Is this your way of getting revenge?' De Niro, in an elaborate gesture, shakes his head fourteen times quickly before he replies 'no …', and then, in a smaller arc (like a physical reverberation or aftershock), shakes it ten more times, before he says: 'It's just the way I see things.'

This line is simple, but quietly haunting. Delivered differently, it might have sounded heroic, assertive, triumphant. De Niro offers a low-key reading: Noodles is sticking to his vision of events, obstinately, proudly, even cruelly. In the total scheme of the film, the words trigger a grimmer, still less heroic reflection. Noodles is offering his vision, his perception, his subjective consciousness to us as the final word of this story – as if it had been, all along, his story. But how can Noodles' testament truly comfort us, in a movie which exposes at every turn the fantasies, blind spots, masks and treacheries inherent in a drama of seeing?

Postscript: Ashes of Time

The truth is that I am not a director of action. ... I'm more a director of gestures and silences.

Sergio Leone, 1984[83]

Traces of Leone's bold, vulgar, expressionistic legacy are everywhere in contemporary cinema. In 1995 Sam Raimi's *The Quick and the Dead* and Robert Rodriguez's *Desperado* proudly mimicked, with no small amount of comic verve, the stylistic mannerisms of Leone's Westerns. In a subtler vein, Eric Rochant – who avows having repeatedly viewed and studied *Once Upon a Time in America* – structured his political thriller *Les Patriotes* (1995) entirely upon the device of the 'reveal'. And those grand, wordless, revelatory clinches that Leone did so well – where the feel of an epic is captured in a simple exchange of looks, in frame entries and exits – the spirit and method of these Leonesque moments unmistakeably reappears in key scenes of Michael Mann's *The Last of the Mohicans* (1992) and Clint Eastwood's *The Bridges of Madison County* (1995).

Leone's favourite themes, as well as his forms, return. John Woo's grandiloquent and spectacular action films, such as *The Killer* (1989) and *Hard Boiled* (1992), have revived Leone's taste for epic, bloody tales of virile friendship. There are strong, extensive traces of the Leone 'feel' in Danny DeVito's directorial work – especially *Hoffa* (1992), which shouldn't surprise us considering that the character of Jimmy in *Once Upon a Time in America*, and the association of death with a large, ominous truck, were inspired by the real-life story of Hoffa. And, in its brittle, garish, maudlin way, *Toto the Hero* (Jaco van Dormael, 1991) recycles Leone's fascination with 'stolen lives' and a deadly male rivalry spanning childhood and old age.

There is a notable Leone influence on the current 'Tarantino generation' of film-makers, just as there was on a previous generation of 'movie brats' (Coppola, De Palma, Kaufman, Scorsese, Cimino, Carpenter) who, according to Bernardo Bertolucci, 'all rediscovered

American cinema through European cinema'.[84] Many critics have discussed this phenomenon in relation to Leone's oeuvre: the unprecedented 'cultural exchange' which his films inaugurated by offering American (perhaps especially Italo-American) film-making a radical, sometimes subversive reflection of itself, refracted through the

Noodles nervously walks the streets with a suitcase of cash

aesthetic forms and possibilities opened up by the various post-war 'new cinema' movements (e.g., in France, Japan, Brazil, Italy). This is the phenomenon that Noël Simsolo calls Leone's 'American boomerang'.[85]

Once Upon a Time in America offers a particularly acute, poignant moment of retrospection in the cultural history of such boomerang

exchanges in international cinema. As an almost emblematic post-modern hero in the context of early 80s art and culture, Noodles – back from the dead, a sleepwalker, the symbolic vehicle for an 'endgame' reflection on cinema's faded glories – is the precursor of Eastwood's ghostly pale rider (in his 1985 Western of that name); or the solitary Chuck Yeager on his mad flight into the heavens, eclipsed by history in Kaufman's *The Right Stuff* (1983); or Wim Wenders' amnesiac hero appearing abruptly out of a Fordian desert wilderness in *Paris, Texas* (1984): all films which, like Leone's, involve an intense 'auto-reference' to past genres, whether the Western, the war/aviation film, or Hollywood family melodrama. Similarly, in Walter Hill's revisionist Western *Wild Bill* (1995), opium opens for the legendary cowboy hero, as it does for Noodles, a door to retrospection and regret.

The gangster/crime genre, enjoying a renewed momentum since the early 90s, has been particularly affected by Leone's magisterial example. Coppola's *The Godfather, Part III* (1990), Ferrara's *King of New York* (1990), Phil Joanou's *State of Grace* (1990), Barry Levinson's *Bugsy* (1991), Robert Benton's *Billy Bathgate* (1991), De Palma's *Carlito's Way* (1993), Mann's *Heat* (1995) and Walter Hill's *Last Man Standing* (1996) – all of these films bear the mark of Leone's fatalism, his melancholy, his sombre pictorial strategies and funeral rhythms (and several have powerful scores by Morricone). The gangster hero becomes, more than ever, a type of phantom or zombie haunted by betrayal, and the inevitability of his own demise. He is the last action hero, frozen in immobility as the entire grand machine of epic gangster narrative winds down and splutters out around him: witness Christopher Walken in *King of New York*, the man who cries 'I don't need forever!', simply giving out in the back of a taxi in the final moments of the film, his gun-holding hand suddenly lifeless.

The ashes of time and of romance, and those telling 'gestures and silences' with which Leone narrated the tale of Noodles, are found strewn all over the gangster genre today: in the love of Don Corleone (Al Pacino) for his daughter (Sofia Coppola), gunned down before his eyes; in the violently interrupted escape route to a better life undertaken by ex-gangster Carlito (Pacino again) and the woman (Penelope Ann Miller) carrying their child; in the devastating, wordless clinch in which a master criminal (De Niro) must simply turn and walk away from his lover because he sees the 'heat coming around the corner'. And there is De Niro once more as a Jewish criminal without glory at the end of Scorsese's *Casino* (1996) – a film that reunites the star with James Woods – whose character is old, unglamorous, counting out his days.

But *Once Upon a Time in America*'s male pathos, its wintry air of romance, its hollowed-out narrative structure, and its apocalyptic mood – these qualities radiate out far beyond the film's nominal genre. The echoes are evident in Eastwood's *Bird* (1988), the chronologically scrambled biopic of Charlie Parker, and his Western masterpiece *Unforgiven* (1992), another story of masculine 'original sin' which is dedicated to Leone and Don Siegel. These echoes can also be heard, transposed in various ways, in Scorsese's *The Age of Innocence* (1993), Woo's *Bullet in the Head* (1990), Bertolucci's *The Last Emperor* (1987) and Yves Angelo's *Le Colonel Chabert* (1994). And in Chinese cinema, beyond the case of Woo, almost any epic devoted to social and personal genesis seems to have digested something of the look, design, structure or mood of Leone's film – from Tsui Hark's *Once Upon a Time in China* series to Wong Kar-Wai's near-experimental *Ashes of Time* (1995).

As the example of Wong indicates, Leone's effect upon the realm of art cinema has been steadily noticeable since his death. What Chion praises as the generative contradictions or impurities of *Once Upon a Time in America* – its bold see-sawing between vulgarity and sublimity, its imbrication of detailed historical realities with grand mythic conceits[86] – all these reappear with a gleeful vengeance in Emir Kusturica's *Underground* (1995), which at one stage bore the working title of *Once Upon a Time There was a Country*. Betrayal by history and by those closest to one's skin, the battle of two men over the same woman – these themes pop up, too, in Nikita Mikhalkov's epic *Burnt by the Sun* (1994). A less instantly recognisable, more radical, almost punk re-working of the bold clashes in Leone's style occurs in the work of another of his admirers: Leos Carax (*Les Amants du Pont-Neuf*, 1991).

And finally in *Bitter Moon* (1992), another extremely impure film in every respect, Roman Polanski pays Leone the ultimate, kidding compliment that one great director can pay to another. He has his unlikable male hero (Peter Coyote) watch *Once Upon a Time in America* – the restaurant scene – on TV. It is a comically degraded version: a French dubbed version of the short American cut on a black and white

Age can wither him: Noodles' failing eyesight; yesterday suddenly: Patsy and Dominic set. And, as Morricone's deliberately muzak-like arrangement of 'Amapola' continues to play over Polanski's own scene, he allows the fraught relationship of Noodles and Deborah to provide a mirror to the subsequent sado-masochistic emotional tangle between his own starring couple (Coyote and Emmanuelle Seigner): modern lovers stranded, like Leone's, between innocence and decadence, between sentimental yearning and nihilistic despair.

Notes

1 Quoted in 'Once Upon Another Time', author anonymous, *Films Illustrated* vol. 11 no. 124, January 1982, p. 157.
2 Bill Krohn, 'La Planète Leone', *Cahiers du cinéma* no. 422, July–August 1989, p. 12 (English language original courtesy of the author).
3 Ibid., p. 13.
4 Chris Peachment, 'The World was Yours', *Sight and Sound*, Autumn 1984, p. 301.
5 Krohn, 'La Planète Leone', p. 13.
6 See, for instance, Leone interviewed by Elaine Lomenzo, 'A Fable for Adults', *Film Comment*, August 1984, p. 22.
7 See, for instance, Jean A. Gili, 'Entretien avec Sergio Leone', *Positif* no. 280, June 1984, p. 8.
8 Michel Sineux, 'Sergio Leone: Rêver à l'intérieur du mythe américain', *Positif* no. 340, June 1989, p. 3.
9 Richard T. Jameson, 'Chasing the Hat', *Film Comment*, September–October 1990, p. 32.
10 Don Ranvaud and Alberto Farassino, 'An Interview with Jean-Luc Godard', *Framework* no. 21, Summer 1983, p. 9.
11 Tony Rayns, '*Once Upon a Time in America*', *Monthly Film Bulletin* no. 609, October 1984, p. 296.
12 Raymond Bellour, 'Segmenting/Analysing', in Rick Altman (ed.), *Genre: The Musical* (London: Routledge & Kegan Paul, 1981), p. 108.
13 Vincent Ostria, '*Il Était une fois dans l'Ouest*', *100 Films pour une vidéothèque, Cahiers du cinéma* 'hors-série', December 1993, p. 67.
14 Serge Toubiana, '*Il Était une fois en Amérique', 100 Films pour une vidéothèque*, p. 68.
15 See Stephen Heath, *Questions of Cinema* (London: Macmillan, 1981).
16 Leone interviewed by Pete Hamill, '*Once Upon a Time in America*', *American Film*, June 1984, p. 23.
17 Ibid., p. 25.
18 See Gili, 'Entretien', p. 8.
19 This information derives from Rayns, '*Once Upon a Time*', p. 297.
20 Hamill, '*Once Upon a Time*', p. 23.
21 Ibid.
22 Stuart Kaminsky, correspondence with author, December 1995.
23 Harry Grey, *The Hoods* (New York: Crown Publishers, 1952). Republished as *Once Upon a Time in America* (London: Bloomsbury, 1997).
24 Gili, 'Entretien', p. 7.
25 Hamill, '*Once Upon a Time'*, p. 23.
26 David Thomson, *A Biographical Dictionary of Film* (London: André Deutsch, 1994), p. 438.
27 Hamill, '*Once Upon a Time'*, p. 24.
28 Michel Chion, 'Il y a un lieu, l'Amerique', *Cahiers du cinéma* no. 359, May 1984, p. 13.
29 Meaghan Morris, 'Art is the Villain in this Sprawling Saga', *Australian Financial Review*, 12 October 1984, p. 47.
30 Brian Case, 'Remembrance of Things Pasta', *Stills*, November 1984, p. 56.
31 Noël Simsolo, *Conversations avec Sergio Leone*, (Paris: Stock/Cinéma, 1987), p. 163.
32 Sergio Leone, 'Il Était une fois …', *Cahiers du cinéma* no. 422, July–August 1989, p. 19; this is a French translation of the introduction to Marcello Garofalo, *Once Upon a Time in America: Photographic Memories* (Rome: Editalia, 1984).
33 Rayns, '*Once Upon a Time'*, p. 297.
34 Jacques Rivette, 'Interview on *Out*', in J. Rosenbaum (ed.), *Rivette: Texts and Interviews* (London: British Film Institute, 1978), p. 51.

35 Quoted in Jean-Philippe Domecq, 'Reflets dans un saxo d'or', *Positif* no. 280, June 1984, p. 2. Original reference is *Le Point*, January 1984. Cf. also Leone, 'A main armée', *Positif* no. 280, June 1984, pp. 16–18. This is the director's introduction to the Italian edition of *The Hoods*.
36 Robert Warshow, *The Immediate Experience: Movies, Comics, Theatre and Other Aspects of Popular Culture* (New York: Athenium, 1970), pp. 127–33. See also Rolando Caputo, '*Once Upon a Time in America*', *Tension* no. 5, October 1984, pp. 9–10.
37 Warshow, 'Movie Chronicle: *The Westerner*', *The Immediate Experience*, p. 136.
38 Morris, 'Art is the Villain', p. 47.
39 Gilles Deleuze, *Cinema 1: The Movement-Image* (Minneapolis: University of Minnesota Press, 1986) and *Cinema 2: The Time-Image* (Minneapolis: University of Minnesota Press, 1989).
40 See William D. Routt, 'Todorov Among the Gangsters', *Art & Text* no. 34, Spring 1989, pp. 109–26.
41 See Peter Wollen, 'The Hermeneutic Code', *Readings and Writings: Semiotic Counter-Strategies* (London: Verso, 1982), pp. 40–8.
42 For a fuller discussion, see my 'Mr Big', *Stuffing*, film genre issue, 1987, pp. 50–77.
43 Rainer Maria Rilke, *On Love and Other Difficulties* (New York: W.W. Norton, 1975), p. 36.
44 Krohn, 'La Planète Leone', p. 13.
45 Sue Adler, 'Ennio Morricone', *Cinema Papers* no. 49, December 1984, p. 427.
46 Leone's presentation of Noodles' confused attitude to these contrasting 'feminine archetypes' in his life is strikingly prefigured in a passage of Grey's novel: 'I was looking up at Dolores, who was gazing out of her window across the street. … I stood there daydreaming about her. My first love …. Then my thoughts wandered off to Peggy. A new strange inner excitement overwhelmed me' (*Once Upon a Time in America*, p. 37).
47 Stuart Kaminsky, 'Narrative Time in Sergio Leone's *Once Upon a Time in America*', in R. Barton Palmer (ed.), *The Cinematic Text: Methods and Approaches* (New York: AMS Press, 1989), p. 89.
48 Lesley Stern, *The Scorsese Connection* (London: British Film Institute, 1995), p. 216.
49 This draft of the script is undated, but clearly derives from the 1981–2 period involving Kaminsky, since much of the dialogue is identical to that which appears in the film. It carries a sole, mysterious credit: 'English Version by David Mills.'
50 Kaminsky, 'Narrative Time', p. 92.
51 Jacques Rivette et al., 'Montage', in Rosenbaum (ed.), *Rivette: Texts and Interviews*, p. 87.
52 See Jonathan Rosenbaum, '*Gertrud* as Nonnarrative: The Desire for the Image', *Placing Movies: The Practice of Criticism* (Berkeley: University of California Press, 1995), p. 112.
53 Rolando Caputo, '*Once Upon a Time in America*', *Cinema Papers* no. 49, December 1984, p. 459.
54 Serge Daney, 'Falling Out of Love', *Sight and Sound*, July 1992, p. 16.
55 Both quotes from Adam Knee, 'Notions of Authorship and the Reception of *Once Upon a Time in America*', *Film Criticism* vol. X no. 1, Fall 1985, p. 7.
56 Mary Corliss, 'Once Upon a Time …', *Film Comment*, August 1984, p. 19.
57 Ibid., p. 20.
58 Ibid., p. 21.
59 The speculation in the American press over the the merits of a short version of *Once Upon a Time in America*, and its possible superiority over Leone's cut, mercifully ended

when the latter finally received a limited American re-release, partly due to pressure from critics, in October 1984 – with Pauline Kael, among major reviewers, publicly re-assessing the film more favourably. See the essay 'Tidal' in Kael's *State of the Art* (New York: E.P. Dutton, 1985), pp. 359–64.
60 See note 49.
61 Michel Chion, Serge Le Péron and Serge Toubiana, 'Entretien avec Sergio Leone', *Cahiers du cinéma* no. 359, May 1984, p. 7.
62 Ibid.
63 Draft script, pp. 221-2.
64 In the draft script, Eve is in fact not killed at the very start of the film, but allowed to live into a sad, old age. Carol in the nursing home narrates Eve's backstory, how she waited for years for Noodles' return, and then calmly committed suicide by an overdose of pills.
65 Ronnie Scheib, 'Images in Exile', *American Film*, March 1985, p. 31.
66 Laura Mulvey, *Visual and Other Pleasures* (Bloomington: Indiana University Press, 1989), p. 25.
67 Stan Brakhage, 'The 60th Birthday Interview', *Film Culture* no. 78, Summer 1994, p. 35.
68 Hamill, '*Once Upon a Time*', p. 26.
69 *Jean-Claude Carrière*, British TV documentary presented by Melvyn Bragg and directed by David Thomas, 1994.
70 Draft script, p. 301.
71 Gili, 'Entretien', p. 14.
72 Kaminsky, 'Narrative Time', p. 85.
73 Raymond Bellour, 'Le film qu'on accompagne', *Trafic* no. 4, Autumn 1992, p. 128.
74 Director's note dated 1981, quoted in Kaminsky, 'Narrative Time', pp. 98–9.
75 Ibid., p. 93.
76 Ibid., p. 97. Cf. also Caputo, '*Once Upon a Time*', *Cinema Papers*, p. 459.
77 Lee Hays, *Once Upon a Time in America* (London: Sphere Books, 1984), p. 184.
78 It should be noted – although this is irrelevant to Chion's Freudian interpretation – that according to the dialogue in the dressing room scene, Deborah is not in fact David's mother (as many commentators assume). He is Max's child from an earlier marriage.
79 Michel Chion, 'Il y a un lieu', pp. 12–13.
80 Ibid., p. 12.
81 Gili, 'Entretien', p. 8.
82 Rayns, '*Once Upon a Time*', p. 296.
83 Hamill, '*Once Upon a Time*', p. 25.
84 Bertolucci, 'Once Upon a Time in Italy', *Film Comment*, July–August 1989, p. 78.
85 Simsolo, 'Sergio Leone ou l'Amérique-boomerang', *Autrement* no. 79, 1986, pp. 208–10; cf. also Krohn, 'La Planète Leone', p. 10.
86 Chion, 'Il y a un lieu', p. 13.

Credits

ONCE UPON A TIME IN AMERICA

USA
1983

Copyright
Embassy International Pictures
Production companies
A P. S.O. International Release.
An Arnon Milchan presentation. A film by Sergio Leone
Executive producer
Claudio Mancini
Producer
Arnon Milchan
Executive in charge of production
Fred Caruso
Production supervisor
Mario Cotone
New York production co-ordinator
Gail Kearns
Montreal production manager
Ginette Hardy
Unit manager
Walter Massi
Location managers
Attilio Viti
New York:
Robert Rothbard
Montreal:
Pierre Laberge
New York location controller
Herb Hetzer
New York production liaison
Ted Kurdyla
Consultant to the producer
Robert Benmussa
Production auditor
Gianna Di Michele
Accountants
Fausto Capozzi,
Sergio Rosa,
Diana Di Michele
New York:
Dominique Bruballa
Montreal:
Lucy Drolet
New York production secretaries
Jennifer Wyckoff,
Francesca Alatri
Production assistants
Piero Sassaroli,
Tonino Palombi
Director
Sergio Leone
First assistant director
Fabrizio Sergenti Castellani
New York assistant directors
Dennis Benatar, Amy Wells
Dialogue director
Brian Freilino
Casting
Cis Corman, Joy Todd
Montreal extras casting
Flo Galant, Sylvie Bourque
Screenplay
Leonardo Benvenuti, Piero De Bernardi, Enrico Medioli, Franco Arcalli, Franco Ferrini, Sergio Leone.
Based on the novel *The Hoods* by Harry Grey
Additional dialogue
Stuart Kaminsky
Director of photography
Tonino Delli Colli
Cameraman
Carlo Tafani
Camera assistants
Antonio Scaramuzza,
Sandro Battaglia
New York assistant cameraman
Crescenzo Notarile
Gaffers
Romano Mancini
New York:
John Newby
Montreal:
Walter Kymkiw
Key grips
Augusto Diamanti
New York:
Steve Baker
Montreal:
Normand Guy
Stillman
Angelo Novi
Montreal special effects
Gabe Vidella, Special Effects Unit, Hollywood
Montreal special effects assistant
Louis Craig
Editor
Nino Baragli
Editing co-ordinator
Maurizio Mancini
First assistant editor
Vivi Tonini

Assistant editors
Ornella Chistolini, Patrizia Cerasani, Alessandro Baragli, Giorgio Venturoli
Art directors
Carlo Simi
New York:
James Singelis
Set designer
Giovanni Natalucci
New York set decorator
Gretchen Rau
Set dressers
Bruno Cesari, Osvaldo Desideri
Construction co-ordinators
Tullio Lullo
New York:
Joey Litto
Swing gang
Nello Giorgetti
New York set builders
Otto Jacoby, George Messaris
New York scenic chargeperson
Elouise Meyer
Montreal scenic painter
Alain Giguere
Montreal chief carpenter
Claude Simard
Propmaster
Gianni Fiumi
Prop men
New York:
Steve Kerschoff
Montreal:
Ronald Fauteux
Costume designers
Gabriella Pescucci
New York Associate:
Richard Bruno
Assistant costume designers
Raffaella Leone, Marina Frassine
New York costumer
Helen Butler
Wardrobe costumes
Umberto Tirelli
Makeup department
Nilo Jacoponi, Manlio Rocchetti, Gino Zamprioli
New York dental make-up
Henry R. Dwork, DDS
Hair department
Maria Teresa Corridoni, Renata Magnanti, Enzo Cardella
New York make-up/hair
Randy Coronato
Wigs
Rocchetti - Carboni
Titles/optical effects
Studio 4
Music/music director
Ennio Morricone
Music performed by
Unione Musicisti di Roma Symphony Orchestra
Flute de Pan:
Gheorghe Zamfir
Music recording mixer
Sergio Marcotulli
Additional music
'God Bless America' by Irving Berlin, performed by Kate Smith; 'Summertime' from 'Porgy and Bess' by George Gershwin, Dubose Heyward, Ira Gershwin; 'Night and Day' by Cole Porter; 'Yesterday' by John Lennon, Paul McCartney; 'Amapola' by Joseph M. La Calle, (English Lyrics) Albert Gamse; 'La gazza ladra' by Gioacchino Rossini, directed by Francesco Molinari Pradelli
Mixers
Jean Pierre Ruh, Fausto Ancillai
Boom man
Bruno Charrier
Sound effects
Cooperativa di Produzione e Lavoro Studio Sound a.r.l, Cine Audio Effects s.r.l.
Dubbing editor
Roberto Rietti
Post-sync editors
Nicholas Stevenson, Gabrio Astori
New York ADR sound
Paul Zydel
Stunt co-ordinator
Benito Stefanelli
Transportation
Romana Transporti Cinematografici
New York transportation captain
James Giblin
New York antique car co-ordinator
Sonny Abagnale
New York unit publicist
Bruce Bahrenburg

Robert De Niro
David 'Noodles' Aaronson
James Woods
Maximilian 'Max' Bercovicz/ 'Christopher Bailey'
Elizabeth McGovern
Deborah
Treat Williams
James 'Jimmy' Conway O'Donnell

Tuesday Weld
Carol
Burt Young
Joe
Joe Pesci
Frankie Minoldi
Danny Aiello
Police Chief Aiello
William Forsythe
Philip 'Cockeye' Stein
James Hayden
Patrick 'Patsy' Goldberg
Darlanne Fleugel
Eve
Larry Rapp
Fat Moe
Dutch Miller
Van Linden
Robert Harper
Sharkey
Richard Bright
Chicken Joe
Gerard Murphy
Crowning
Amy Ryder
Peggy
Olga Carlatos
Woman in the puppet theatre
Mario Brega
Mandy
Ray Dittrich
Trigger
Frank Gio
Beefy
Karen Shallo
Mrs Aiello
Angelo Florio
Willie the Ape
Scott Tiler
Young 'Noodles'
Rusty Jacobs
Young Max/David Bailey
Brian Bloom
Young 'Patsy'
Adrian Curran
Young 'Cockeye'
Mike Monetti
Young Fat Moe
Noah Moazezi
Dominic
James Russo
Bugsy
Frankie Caserta
Joey Marzella
Bugsy's gang
Clem Caserta
Al Capuano
Frank Sisto
Fred Capuano
Jerry Strivelli
Johnny Capuano
Julie Cohen
Young Peggy
Marvin Scott
TV interviewer
Mike Gendel
Irving Gold
Paul Herman
Monkey
Ann Neville
Girl in coffin
Joey Faye
Adorable old man
Linda Ipanema
Nurse Thompson
Tandy Cronin
First reporter
Richard Zobel
Second reporter
Baxter Harris
Third reporter
Arnon Milchan
Chauffeur
Bruno Iannone
Thug
Marty Licata
Cemetery caretaker
Marcia Jean Kurtz
Max's mother
Estelle Harris
Peggy's mother
Richard Foronji
Whitey
Gerritt Debeer
Drunk
Jennifer Connelly
Young Deborah
Margherita Pace
Body double for young Deborah
Alexander Godfrey
News-stand man
Cliff Cudney
Mounted policeman
Paul Farentino
Second mounted policeman
Bruce Bahrenburg
Sergeant Halloran
Mort Freeman
Street singer
Sandra Solberg
Friend of young Deborah
Jay Zeely
Foreman
Massimo Liti
Young Marco

20,549 feet
228 minutes
In colour

Credits compiled by Julian Grainger and Markku Salmi, BFI Filmographical Unit.

Bibliography

Adler, Sue, 'Ennio Morricone', *Cinema Papers* no. 49, December 1984.

Anonymous, 'Once Upon Another Time', *Films Illustrated* vol. 11 no. 124, January 1982.

Bellour, Raymond, 'Segmenting/Analysing', in Rick Altman (ed.), *Genre: The Musical* (London: Routledge & Kegan Paul, 1981).

Bellour, Raymond, 'Le film qu'on accompagne', *Trafic* no. 4, Autumn 1992.

Bertolucci, Bernardo, 'Once Upon A Time In Italy', *Film Comment*, July–August 1989.

Brakhage, Stan, 'The 60th Birthday Interview', *Film Culture* no. 78, Summer 1994.

Caputo, Rolando, '*Once Upon a Time in America*', *Cinema Papers* no. 49, December 1984.

Caputo, Rolando, '*Once Upon a Time in America*', *Tension* no. 5, October 1984.

Case, Brian, 'Remembrance of Things Pasta', *Stills*, November 1984.

Chion, Michel, 'Il y a un lieu, l'Amérique', *Cahiers du cinéma* no. 359, May 1984.

Chion, Michel, Serge Le Péron and Serge Toubiana, 'Entretien avec Sergio Leone', *Cahiers du cinéma* no. 359, May 1984.

Corliss, Mary, 'Once Upon a Time … ', *Film Comment*, August 1984.

Deleuze, Gilles, *Cinema 1: The Movement-Image* (Minneapolis: University of Minnesota Press, 1986).

Deleuze, Gilles, *Cinema 2: The Time-Image* (Minneapolis: University of Minnesota Press, 1989).

Daney, Serge, 'Falling Out of Love', *Sight and Sound*, July 1992.

Domecq, Jean-Philippe, 'Reflets dans un saxo d'or', *Positif* no. 280, June 1984.

Garofalo, Marcello, *Once Upon a Time in America: Photographic Memories* (Rome: Editalia, 1984).

Gili, Jean A., 'Entretien avec Sergio Leone', *Positif* no. 280, June 1984.

Grey, Harry, *The Hoods* (New York: Crown Publishers, 1952). Republished as *Once Upon a Time in America* (London: Bloomsbury, 1997).

Hamill, Pete, '*Once Upon a Time in America*', *American Film*, June 1984.

Hays, Lee, *Once Upon a Time in America* (London: Sphere Books, 1984).

Heath, Stephen, *Questions of Cinema* (London: Macmillan, 1981).

Jameson, Richard T., 'Chasing the Hat', *Film Comment*, September–October 1990.

Kael, Pauline, *State of the Art* (New York: E.P. Dutton, 1985).

Kaminsky, Stuart M., 'Narrative Time in Sergio Leone's *Once Upon a Time in America*', in R. Barton Palmer (ed.), *The Cinematic Text: Methods and Approaches* (New York: AMS Press, 1989).

Knee, Adam, 'Notions of Authorship and the Reception of *Once Upon a Time in America*', *Film Criticism*, vol. X no. 1, Fall 1985.

Krohn, Bill, 'La Planète Leone', *Cahiers du cinéma* no. 422, July–August 1989.

Leone, Sergio, 'A main armée', *Positif* no. 280, June 1984.

Leone, Sergio, 'Il était une fois … ', *Cahiers du cinéma* no. 422, July–August 1989.

Lomenzo, Elaine, 'A Fable for Adults', *Film Comment*, August 1984.

Martin, Adrian, 'Mr Big', *Stuffing*, film genre issue, 1987.

Morris, Meaghan, 'Art is the Villain in this Sprawling Saga', *Australian Financial Review*, 12 October 1984.

Mulvey, Laura, *Visual and Other Pleasures* (Bloomington: Indiana University Press, 1989).

Ostria, Vincent, '*Il était une fois dans l'Ouest*', *100 Films pour une vidéothèque*, *Cahiers du cinéma* 'hors-série', December 1993.
Peachment, Chris, 'The World Was Yours', *Sight and Sound*, Autumn 1984.
Ranvaud, Don and Farassino, Alberto, 'An Interview with Jean-Luc Godard', *Framework* no. 21, Summer 1983.
Rayns, Tony, '*Once Upon a Time in America*', *Monthly Film Bulletin* no. 609, October 1984.
Rilke, Rainer Maria, *On Love and Other Difficulties* (New York: W.W. Norton, 1975).
Rosenbaum, Jonathan, (ed.), *Rivette: Texts and Interviews* (London: British Film Institute, 1978).
Rosenbaum, Jonathan, *Placing Movies: The Practice of Criticism* (Berkeley: University of California Press, 1995).
Routt, William D., 'Todorov Among the Gangsters', *Art & Text* no. 34, Spring 1989.
Scheib, Ronnie, 'Images in Exile', *American Film*, March 1985.
Simsolo, Noël, 'Sergio Leone ou l'Amérique-boomerang', *Autrement* no. 79, 1986.
Simsolo, Noël, *Conversations avec Sergio Leone* (Paris: Stock/Cinéma, 1987).
Sineux, Michel, 'Rêver à l'intérieur du mythe américain', *Positif* no. 340, June 1989.
Stern, Lesley, *The Scorsese Connection* (London: British Film Institute, 1995).
Thomson, David, *A Biographical Dictionary of Film* (London: André Deutsch, 1994).
Toubiana, Serge, '*Il Était une fois en Amérique*', *100 Films pour une vidéothèque*, *Cahiers du cinéma* 'hors-série', December 1993.
Warshow, Robert, *The Immediate Experience: Movies, Comics, Theatre and Other Aspects of Popular Culture* (New York: Athenium, 1970).
Wollen, Peter, *Readings and Writings: Semiotic Counter-Strategies* (London: Verso, 1982).

BFI Publishing
21 Stephen Street
FREEPOST 7
LONDON
W1E 4AN